Understanding
Christian Apologetics

"As we slide deeper into post-Christendom, it is vital for us to avoid hiding out within the comfortable confines of our own apologetics echo chambers. *Understanding Christian Apologetics* will help you venture out into conversations with those who dwell in different apologetics rooms. While I find some of these rooms sturdier than others, I don't believe any single room (i.e., apologetics system) can by itself contain the riches of God's revelation. Hence, we need the kind of critical engagement, fresh retrievals, and creative proposals represented by this book's contributors so that together we might always be reforming by God's never-changing word while wisely engaging in an ever-changing world."

–Joshua Chatraw, Billy Graham Chair of Evangelism and Cultural Engagement, Beeson Divinity School

"*Understanding Christian Apologetics* is an accessible yet challenging exploration of five key approaches to defending the faith. This survey of apologetic methods–including the often overlooked cultural and ecclesial approaches–stands out as a model of charitable dialogue. The authors exemplify the kind of respectful engagement so needed in the church today. A fantastic resource for Christians beginning their study of apologetics!"

–Mikel Del Rosario, professor of Bible and Theology, Moody Bible Institute

"For those wanting to dive deep and finely parse the details of apologetics methodology, *Understanding Christian Apologetics* is the book for you! In the introduction to the book, Timothy Paul Jones gives a wonderful and broad exploration of the many approaches to the discipline. Each contributor then makes clear and interesting arguments for their respective views, followed by respectful but forceful engagement in each contributors' response. I suspect this will immediately become the go-to source for students interested in working out their methodological approach to Christian apologetics."

–Travis Dickinson, professor of philosophy, Dallas Baptist University

"To be a disciple of Jesus invariably means being his witness in spirit and word. So Timothy Paul Jones is exactly right in his introduction when he claims, 'The question is not whether we will do apologetics; it is whether we will do apologetics well.' He's exactly right, and a careful reader of this book will be especially well resourced to think more clearly about the theological and missional dimensions of apologetics."

–Matthew J. Hall, provost, Biola University

"*Understanding Christian Apologetics* facilitates a fresh and nuanced conversation on the diverse ways Christians have thought about the task of apologetic ministry, both past and present. Readers will find an accessible articulation and defense of five distinct yet often overlapping perspectives on how the church can work, in the words of twentieth-century missionary-apologist Lesslie Newbigin, to cultivate a 'missionary encounter with Western culture.' By including the Cultural Apologetic and the Ecclesial Apologetic perspectives, *Understanding Christian Apologetics* showcases recent developments in the discipline and helpfully moves the conversation forward. It will serve as a clear and reliable guide for teachers, students, and practitioners of Christian apologetics for years to come."

–Ross D. Inman, associate professor of philosophy, Southeastern Baptist Theological Seminary, and editor-in-chief, *Philosophia Christi*

"*Understanding Christian Apologetics* is a treasure that beautifully captures the essence of what defending the faith is all about–persuading a lost and dying world that Christianity is not only true but beneficial. Each contributor does a phenomenal job of making the case for the strengths and weaknesses of the various approaches, demonstrating that apologists across the spectrum all have something unique and valuable to bring to the table."

–Miss Tytus Jones, urban apologist

"You will be strengthened by this fresh round of helpful debates on the vital topic of apologetic methodology. You will be pleased to know the participants are practitioners, not merely theorists. The writers are respectful–yet clear–in the midst of their disagreements. Personally, I love the visually appealing layout and design–a major bonus to this high-quality work."

–Vocab Malone, Street Apologist Ministries

"*Understanding Christian Apologetics* offers a nuanced and insightful exploration of the varied approaches Christians employ to articulate and defend their faith. Instead of positioning apologetic methods as competing ideologies, the authors skillfully illuminate their unique strengths, fostering a thoughtful and integrative perspective. What particularly resonated with me was the book's consistent emphasis on clarity and charitable engagement. It masterfully models an apologetic rooted in humility, love, and a deep sensitivity to the listener, a crucial element often overlooked."

–Mary Jo Sharp, founder of Confident Christianity Apologetics Ministry, and author of *Why I Still Believe: A Former Atheist's Reckoning with the Bad Reputation Christians Give a Good God*

Understanding *Christian Apologetics*

5 METHODS *for* DEFENDING *the* FAITH

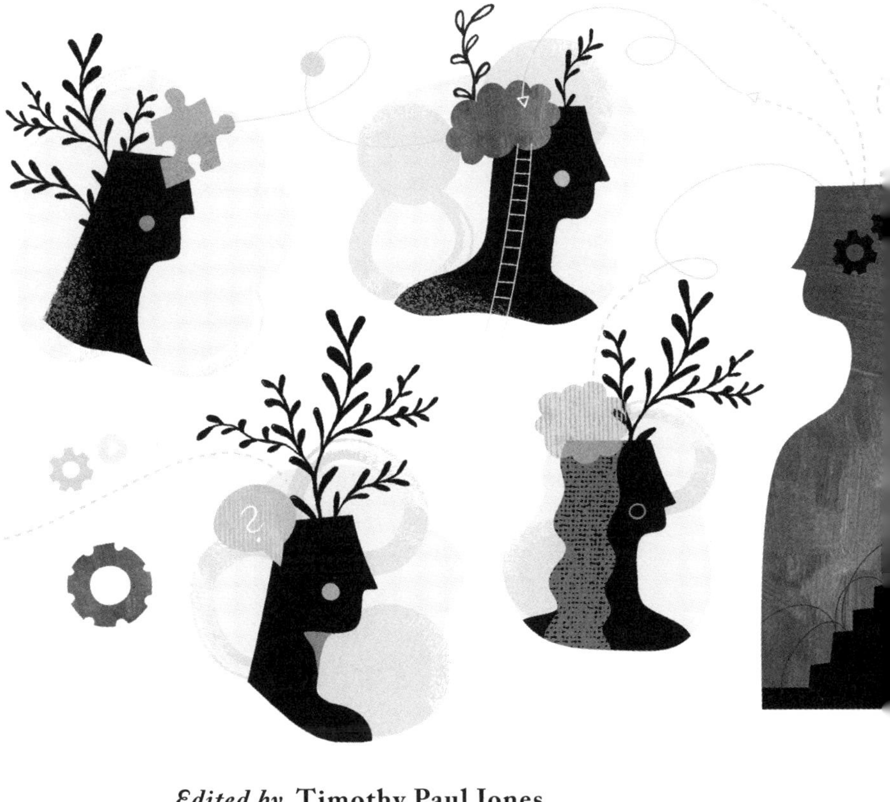

Edited by Timothy Paul Jones

Understanding Christian Apologetics: Five Methods for Defending the Faith

Published by Hendrickson Publishers
3 Centennial Drive
Peabody, Massachusetts 01960
ISBN 978-1-4964-8813-8
www.hendricksonpublishers.com

ISBN 978-1-4964-8813-8 (print)
ISBN 978-1-4964-8815-2 (e-book)
ISBN 978-1-4964-8814-5 (e-book Kindle)
ISBN 978-1-4964-8816-9(e-book Apple)

This book is published in association with Nappaland Literary Agency, an independent firm dedicated to publishing works that are: Authentic. Relevant. Eternal. Visit us on the web at http://www.NappalandLiterary.com.

Cover and title page illustrations by iStock.com/DrAfter123.
Cover design by Karol Bailey.

Printed in the United States of America

First Printing — August 2025

Contents

Foreword

I am grateful to the contributors to this volume for their efforts to help the body of Christ seriously consider how we are to faithfully "contend for the faith once delivered to the saints" (Jude 3) in the modern world. Their readings of the Scriptures, church history, and contemporary culture have borne fruit to encourage and further equip us to defend and commend the good news of Jesus Christ in the time and places that God, according to his good and wise providence, has placed us. I used to come to works like this hoping to find the apologetic "silver bullet." That's no longer the case because I don't believe it exists. I've also come to think that when we believe we have found this mythical "silver bullet," we can become more occupied with defending *it* than the Christian faith. In our zeal to protect our cherished approach, we can all too easily attack anyone who would threaten it by way of question or critique. Having witnessed that (and, to my shame, having participated in it), I was refreshed to find no signs of that spirit between this book's covers.

The manner in which we defend the Christian faith should itself be part of our defense. *How* we offer our apologetic answers is at least as important as the answers we offer. As the apostle Peter reminds us in his call that we always be prepared to make a defense to anyone asking about the reason for our hope, we are to do so with gentleness and respect (1 Pet 3:15). It is the height of inconsistency to call ourselves Christians defending the message about our Lord Jesus Christ in a manner contrary to his character. Thus, what I am most grateful to this volume's contributors for is their example of conversing with those with whom we might at times have strong disagreements, whether they are members of the household of faith or those yet outside. I hope readers will follow that example. I have grieved over the disrespectful and unloving ways Christians have publicly displayed contentious, quarrelsome, and unloving treatment toward one another, sometimes while discussing issues of apologetics and cultural engagement. Brothers and sisters, this ought not to be! I agree with Francis Schaeffer who—while committing himself to offering "honest answers to honest questions"—called demonstrable love and unity between believers the "final apologetic."

Keith Plummer, PhD
Dean of the School of Divinity
Cairn University

Introduction

We Are All Apologists Now

Timothy Paul Jones

"We are all apologists now." When Os Guinness made this claim in *Fool's Talk*, his point was that digital interconnectedness and social media have transformed an overwhelming percentage of the population into public promoters of products—and, in most cases, "our leading product is Us." "We are all apologists now," Guinness declared, "if only on behalf of 'the Daily Me.'"[1] The proof of his words is as near as your smartphone and as endless as your social media feeds. Yet his words ring true in another sense as well.

At one time, the overwhelming majority of people in Western contexts assumed the social benefits of Christianity. Even if the truth of the creeds was questioned and the ethical expectations of the church were ignored, the positive impact of Christian faith was generally taken for granted. This supposition has taken a variety of forms over the centuries. In premodern times, the bonds of society were so entwined with the church that social existence was unimaginable apart from faith. In the early decades of modernity, Christian piety was increasingly perceived as a means of promoting civility.[2] And yet, even as the perceived utility of faith and piety shifted, Christianity was still assumed to be good for the world.

Today, a series of cultural and societal changes has fragmented any widespread perception of an overarching order, grounded in sacred reality,

1. Os Guinness, *Fool's Talk: Recovering the Lost Art of Christian Persuasion* (InterVarsity Press, 2015), 15.

2. Charles Taylor, *A Secular Age* (Harvard University Press, 2007), 43, 103–4.

by which we make sense of our lives. Public spheres have become more secular, and private spheres have grown less similar. When it comes to religious beliefs and moral values, the condition of secularity has disembedded any widely shared notions of a well-ordered cosmos in which social and personal identities are grounded in transcendent reality.[3] Particularly in connection with gender and sexuality, the historic Christian ethic is no longer perceived as beneficial to society.[4]

METAPHYSICS

(from Greek *meta*, beyond + *physika*, natural things)

Branch of philosophy that deals with first principles that are not empirically accessible, including abstract concepts such as being and causation.

One result of this societal shift is that every Christian—regardless of location or vocation—must be prepared to provide reasons for our choice to live in a manner that's consistent with the historic Christian faith. Defending the faith has become an unavoidable consequence of living publicly as a Christian, not just for apologists but for all of us.

We are all apologists now.

The question is not whether we will do apologetics; it is whether we will do apologetics well. And yet, what does it mean to do apologetics well in a secular age? How relevant are past methods and approaches? And how might these methods metamorphose to meet the challenges of the present moment? Those are the questions that this book explores.

Understanding Christian Apologetics is not an apologetics book written to defend the faith; rather, it's an amicable debate about how the faith ought to be defended. Five primary contributors have partnered together to present five distinct perspectives on defending Christian faith and life

---

3. Guinness, *Fool's Talk*, 22–23; Taylor, *Secular Age*, 26, 146; Charles Taylor, *Modern Social Imaginaries* (Duke University Press, 2004), 51–56; Carl Trueman, *The Rise and Triumph of the Modern Self: Cultural Amnesia, Expressive Individualism, and the Road to Sexual Revolution* (Crossway, 2020), 81–83.

4. For the perceived incompatibility of Christian ethics with civic flourishing, see, e.g., the response of a British tribunal when British physician David Mackereth declined to use pronouns that conflicted with an individual's birth gender. The tribunal upheld the termination of his employment because "belief in Genesis 1:27, lack of belief in transgenderism[,] and conscientious objection to transgenderism . . . are incompatible with human dignity," Iliana Magda, "He Opposed Using Transgender Clients' Pronouns. It Became a Legal Battle," *New York Times*, October 3, 2019, https://www.nytimes.com. The perceived opposition between civic good and a Christian understanding of reality may also be observed in *United States v. Windsor*, 570 U.S. 744 (2013). In this decision, religious resistance related to same-sex marriage is reduced to an indication of personal prejudice intended to place "a stigma upon" homosexual persons.

in a secular age. Although every contributor agrees that Scripture is the absolute truth and final authority in all matters of life and faith, each individual takes a different perspective when it comes to the best way to defend this truth.

In each phase of this debate, one contributor kicks off the conversation by pulling together past precedents from Scripture and church history to make a case for their preferred method of apologetics. Fellow contributors then provide a series of cordial critiques that consider the strengths and weaknesses of each perspective, focusing on each method's faithfulness to Scripture as well as its capacity to sustain a relevant and rational defense of Christian doctrine in a secular age.

For many of you, *Understanding Christian Apologetics* is your introduction to the academic discipline of apologetics. If that's you, then welcome to the conversation! I'm delighted you chose this book as your first apologetics text. If terms such as "classical apologetics" and "cultural apologetics," "presuppositionalist" and "evidentialist" (and perhaps even "apologetics" itself!) are new to you, don't be intimidated. I'll be defining key terms in the next section, and I'll sprinkle further definitions throughout the book each time someone introduces a new concept.

A few of you reading this book may be in an altogether different place. You may have read dozens of apologetics and theology books over the past few years, and you're already familiar with the key terms and concepts. If that's you, then I'm grateful you've included this book in your study.

When Is an Apology Not an Apology?

Years ago, the band R.E.M. recorded a song titled "The Apologist" on their album *Up*, with lyrics that hint at a widespread ambiguity related to words such as *apologetics* and *apologist*. The vocalist in "The Apologist" assumes the persona of someone who claims he is "sorry, so sorry" about the monstrous abuses he's committed, but he simultaneously seems to be defending his deeds as well.[5] This semantic wordplay reminds us that, indeed, "sometimes words have two meanings."[6] An "apology" can describe an expression of remorse, yet the same term may also denote a defense.

5. "The Apologist," by Peter Lawrence Buck, Michael E. Mills, and John Michael Stipe, on R.E.M., *Up*, Temporary Music/Warner Brothers, 1998.

6. "Stairway to Heaven," by Jimmy Page and Robert Plant, on Led Zeppelin, *Led Zepplin IV*, Hipgnosis Songs Group/Warner Brothers, 1971.

So which is it when it comes to the Christian sense of "apologetics" and "apologist"?

Although "apologetics" does derive from the same Greek root word as "apologize," ancient apologies had nothing to do with remorse or regret. According to Aristotle's classic text on rhetoric, the word *apology* (Greek, *apologia*) denoted a legal speech of defense.[7] The authors of the New Testament sometimes used *apologia* in this narrow, legal sense (Acts 25:16; 2 Tim 4:16). Yet they—like other Greek writers before them—also deployed the term to refer more broadly to other types of defenses (Acts 22:1; 2 Cor 7:11). In the writings of Peter and Paul, this function of *apologia* included verbal defenses of the gospel (Phil 1:7, 16; 1 Pet 3:15).

In the second and third centuries, the earliest Christian apologists not only defended the truth of the gospel, but they also debunked false charges leveled by those who sacrificed to the venerable gods of Rome.[8] Over time, "apologetics" developed into a descriptor of the aspect of Christian theology that focuses on the defense and rational justification of Christian faith.[9] Taking into account the uses of *apologia* in Scripture and in church history, here's how I define "apologetics" for the purposes of this book:

APOLOGETICS

(from Greek *apologia*, *apologētikos*)

Defense, speech of defense. In Christian usage, the church's reverent, reasonable, and humble defense of the hope we have in the risen Christ, as this hope has been revealed in God's word and God's world.

Apologetics is the church's reverent, reasonable, and humble defense of the hope we have in the risen Christ, as this hope has been revealed in God's word and God's world.[10]

In Christian usage, apologetics has nothing to do with saying, "I'm sorry for what I did," and everything to do with saying, "I have reasons for what I believe."

---

7. "Δίκης δὲ τὸ μὲν κατηγορία τὸ δ᾽ἀπολογία," Aristotle, "Τέχνης Ρητορικής," in *Art of Rhetoric*, trans. J. H. Freese (Harvard University Press, 2020), 1358b.3 (1.10.3); see also 1368b.1 (1.10.10).

8. For an early Christian response to widespread accusations of atheism, cannibalism, and incest, see Athenagoras of Athens, *Legatio pro Christianis*, ed. Miroslav Marcovich (de Gruyter, 1990), 3.1–15.

9. Alister McGrath, *Christian Theology*, 4th ed. (Blackwell, 2007), 487.

10. "Reasonable," "humble," and "reverent" derive from 1 Peter 3:15, in which Peter called his readers to provide a defense "to anyone who demands from you an *account* of the hope that is in you; yet do it with *gentleness* and *reverence*" (NRSVue; emphasis added).

Why Do Apologetics Methods Matter?

Secularity has turned every Christian into an apologist, and rising skepticism is likely to require stronger reasons for our commitments than our own personal testimonies. Particularly in contexts where Christianity no longer carries positive social capital, we must be prepared to provide rational justifications for our ethics and faith. And yet, the more you share justifications for your beliefs, the more likely you are to find yourself wondering about the best ways to provide these reasons. Which defenses should you provide when, and in what order should you share them? Should you provide a skeptic with reasons to believe in God's existence before moving on to the resurrection of Jesus? When sharing evidence for the historical reliability of the Bible, with what biblical texts is it best to begin? And how should shifts in our cultural contexts change the justifications we provide for our faith?

The good news is that the strength of the gospel doesn't depend on your capacity to answer all these questions. You can—and should!—share the story of God's love on the basis of simple faith in the risen Jesus and sincere gratitude for his saving work. "He lives, he lives, salvation to impart!" the gospel song proclaims and then provides one simple rationale for this belief: "You ask me how I know he lives? He lives within my heart."[11] Such faith is warranted, and it is right for the Christian to declare the truth of the gospel on this basis.[12]

At the same time, a long lineage of earlier Christians has provided us with a deep intellectual heritage that can strengthen our defenses of the faith today. This communion of saints that stands behind us encompasses a vast multiethnic multitude of women and men who thought deeply about the best ways to provide reasons for their hope in Christ. Their theological reflections over the centuries have resulted in a wealth of different apologetics methods.

The primary purpose of this book is to enable you to consider which apologetics methods are most faithful to Scripture and most suitable for your context. Practiced rightly, an apologetics method is simply an organized approach, grounded in a particular set of theological commitments, that guides your presentation of reasons for the hope you have in

11. A. H. Ackley, "He Lives," in *New National Baptist Hymnal* (National Baptist Publishing Board, 1977), 102.

12. Alvin Plantinga, *Warranted Christian Belief* (Oxford University Press, 2000), 241–50.

Christ. If you choose one or two perspectives on apologetics as your own, those methods can provide you with a plan so that you can be more intentional whenever someone asks you to defend the hope, faith, and love you've found in Jesus. In one sense, your practical apologetics method is whatever you do next when you share the gospel and someone rejects it.[13] What this book will help you to do is to develop a deliberate defense that's shaped by God's word and the wisdom of God's people throughout the ages. At their best, apologetics methods aren't weapons for academic disputations and debates; they're rhetorical tools that enable you to explain the good story of God around dinner tables and water coolers, on long flights and subway trains, to everyone from your wide-eyed child to your closed-minded coworker.

The landscape of apologetics has shifted many times over the centuries, but the panorama of apologetics today tends to include four primary territories. Although ancient and medieval precedents can be identified for each of these four methods, the Age of Enlightenment and the rise of modernity have deeply reshaped the present practices of each perspective.[14] The titles of the four territories that dominate the topography of contemporary apologetics are:

- Classical apologetics
- Evidential apologetics
- Presuppositional apologetics
- Cultural apologetics.

Four Primary Perspectives on Apologetics

Classical Apologetics

Two-step method that appeals to arguments from reason and nature to establish God's existence and then defends Christian doctrines based on historical evidences. In traditional modern forms of classical apologetics, proofs for theism precede any appeals to miracles

13. Paraphrased from Ted Cabal, "Defending the Resurrection of Jesus," *Southern Baptist Journal of Theology* 18 (2014): 130.

14. For a summary of the ways in which the Enlightenment altered the character and potential functions of classical apologetics, see Stanley Hauerwas, *With the Grain of the Universe: The Church's Witness and Natural Theology* (Baker, 2013), 24–31.

because, unless God exists, there is no reason to think that a miracle can occur. Modern proponents include Norman Geisler, R. C. Sproul, and Peter Kreeft.

Evidential Apologetics

One-step method that argues for the truth of Christianity and the existence of God through direct appeals to historical evidences that support miracles and fulfilled prophecies, with a particular emphasis on historical evidences for the resurrection of Jesus. Modern proponents include John Warwick Montgomery, Gary Habermas, and Josh McDowell.

Presuppositional apologetics

Method that holds that the fundamental disagreement between Christians and non-Christians lies not at the level of differing facts or evidences but at the level of competing presuppositions about ultimate reality and ultimate authority. Christianity provides the only coherent explanation for human rationality. Cornelius Van Til was a prominent pioneer of modern presuppositionalism. More recent proponents include Greg Bahnsen and K. Scott Oliphint.

Cultural apologetics

Method that responds to critiques and inquiries about the historical Christian faith by using cultural expressions and artifacts to reveal human idolatries and to redirect human affections to Jesus by demonstrating how the story of Jesus fulfills yet subverts cultural ideals. Imaginative apologetics and narrative apologetics are types of cultural apologetics. Contemporary proponents include Tim Keller and Christopher Watkin.

Mapping Classical and Evidential Methods

On the map of apologetics methods below, I've positioned classical and evidential apologetics together as methods that focus on common notions and shared evidence. That's because both methods seek to build a case for Christianity that begins with one or more basic beliefs, necessary truths, shared observations, or historical facts on which the Christian and the non-Christian can agree.

Map of Apologetics Methods[15]

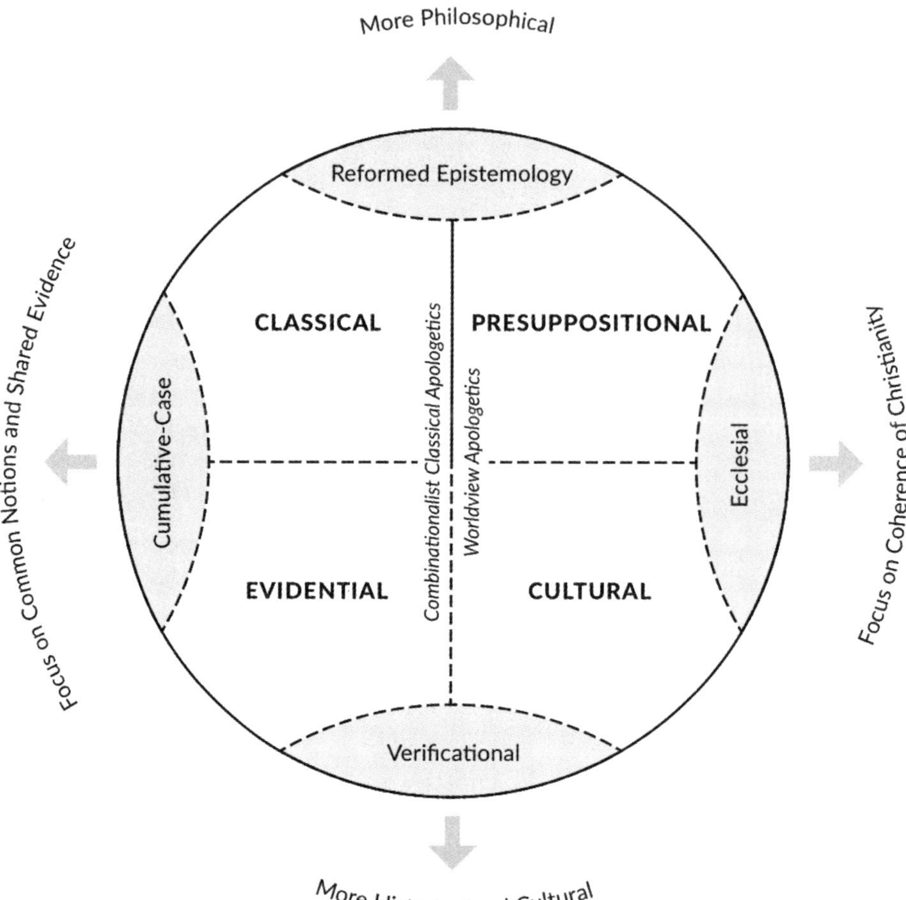

Classical Apologetics

Traditional classical apologists begin their case by establishing a foundation of basic beliefs and necessary truths, such as the law of noncontradiction,

15. Graphic created by Jake Falcone based on lectures and content by Timothy Paul Jones in his Christian Apologetics course at The Southern Baptist Theological Seminary.

the law of causality, and the reliability of sense perception.[16] Many classical apologists move next to classical proofs such as the teleological, tassological, and cosmological arguments, basing their cases for God's existence on the purpose, design, and logic that can be observed throughout the cosmos. Others might seek to show the necessity of God's existence through the ontological argument, a purely rational proof. Some classical apologists add to their case by appealing to evidences from human narratives, morals, conscience, or creativity. Regardless of what arguments a classical apologist uses, the goal is to demonstrate the existence of a supreme divine being. After showing the necessity of theism, classical apologists turn to historical evidences to prove the plausibility of the deity described in the Christian Scriptures.[17]

BASIC BELIEF

A belief that is not inferred from any other belief. A basic belief is properly basic if the individual holding the belief is justified in doing so.

TASSOLOGICAL ARGUMENT

(from Greek *tassō*, arrange)

Proof of God's existence arguing that the appearance of orderly arrangement and design in nature requires the existence of an intelligent designer. Also known as the argument from design.

COSMOLOGICAL ARGUMENT

(from Greek *kosmos*, order)

Classical proof of God's existence arguing that, since all things in the cosmos are caused, there must be an Uncaused Cause who exists independently of the cosmos.

Combinationalist Classical Apologetics

Certain classical apologists—William Lane Craig, for example—don't limit themselves to beginning with classical proofs; they're willing to start with historical or cultural evidences first and then to move toward classical arguments

16. Classical apologetics assumes some form of foundationalism. According to foundationalist theories of epistemic justification, every warranted belief must be either a properly basic belief—a belief that does not depend on any other beliefs and the individual is justified in holding—or a belief inferred from one or more basic beliefs. Strong (classical) foundationalism requires basic beliefs to be indubitable, incorrigible, or infallible. Modest foundationalism distinguishes between having a warranted belief and being able to exhibit the justification of that belief to others; this distinction allows a broader range of beliefs to be treated as basic beliefs. Reformed epistemology applies modest foundationalism to religious epistemology. See William Alston, "Two Types of Foundationalism," *Journal of Philosophy* 73 (1976): 165–85; William Alston, "Has Foundationalism Been Refuted?," *Philosophical Studies* 29 (1976): 287–305; Alvin Plantinga, "Reason and Belief in God," in *Faith and Rationality: Reason and Belief in God,* ed. Alvin Plantinga and Nicholas Wolterstorff (University of Notre Dame Press, 1983), 17, 47–63.

17. R.C. Sproul et al., *Classical Apologetics: A Rational Defense of the Christian Faith and a Critique of Presuppositional Apologetics* (Zondervan, 1984), 70–90, 146–48.

afterward.[18] These individuals might be termed "combinationalist classical apologists" or (to borrow a phrase from Melissa Cain Travis) "holistic classical apologists." Since these apologists may choose to start with historical evidences or with classical proofs, I've identified them on the map by including a pathway titled "combinationalist classical apologetics" that connects the classical and evidential quadrants.

TELEOLOGICAL ARGUMENT
(from Greek *teleō*, complete, accomplish)
Classical proof of God's existence arguing that signs of purpose in the natural world require the existence of a purposeful Creator.

ONTOLOGICAL ARGUMENT
(from Greek *ontos*, being)
Rational proof of God's existence. (1) If God is "That Than Which None Greater Can Be Thought" and (2) if existence in reality is greater than existence in thought alone, then (3) God must therefore exist in reality. If God existed in thought alone, his existence in reality would then be greater than "That Than Which None Greater Can Be Thought," which is absurd because nothing can be greater than greatest.

Evidential Apologetics

Unlike classical apologists, evidential apologists see no need to prove God's existence separately from building a case for the truth of Christianity. Instead of beginning with philosophical arguments, evidential apologists start by turning the spotlight immediately toward texts and artifacts, seeking to demonstrate the historical plausibility of biblical miracles and fulfilled prophecies. According to evidential apologetics, Christians and non-Christians share common ground that includes historical texts and artifacts, sensory data, and rules of inference.[19] Working from texts, historical artifacts, and psychological evidences, the evidential apologist builds a case for Christian faith, typically focusing on evidence for the resurrection of Jesus. Once the truth of the resurrection and the reliability of the Gospels has been established, the evidential apologist shows how the truth of the resurrection supports other essential doctrines such as the deity of Jesus and the authority of Scripture.

Mapping Presuppositional and Cultural Methods

Presuppositional apologetics and cultural apologetics focus less on common foundations and more on the coherence of the Christian faith—which is

18. William Lane Craig, "A Classical Apologist's Closing Remarks," in *Five Views on Apologetics*, ed. Steven Cowan (Zondervan, 2000), 316.
19. Gary Habermas, "Evidential Apologetics," *Five Views*, 97.

why I've grouped these methods together on the opposite side of the map from classical and evidential apologetics. For presuppositional and cultural apologists, the starting point is not a basic belief, necessary truth, or historical artifact that Christians and non-Christians understand in the same way for the same reasons. Instead, it's the recognition that Christianity alone provides a coherent framework for understanding the cosmos we inhabit, the cultures we create, the histories we live, and the stories we tell. Anything coherent in any non-Christian worldview has been borrowed from the understanding of reality that the Triune God has given in his word.

Presuppositional Apologetics

One of the key differences between presuppositional and cultural apologetics has to do with *how* each one unmasks the incoherence of non-Christian perspectives. The emphasis in presuppositional apologetics is more philosophical, frequently focusing on the conflict between Christian and non-Christian epistemologies. According to many presuppositionalists, rationality itself is inexplicable apart from the existence of the Triune God of Scripture. And so, every rational thought that crosses a non-Christian's mind proves the truth of the Triune God of Scripture and reveals the incoherence of rejecting this God. Non-Christian epistemologies are irrational, self-refuting, and ultimately impossible. The presuppositional apologist demonstrates the truth of Christianity by showing that any correct concept the non-Christian knows requires processes of reasoning that are dependent on a Christian conception of reality.

Cultural Apologetics

Cultural apologetics also focuses on the consummate coherence of Christianity, but the cultural apologist highlights this coherence in a different way. Instead of centering their attention on a clash of epistemologies, cultural apologists work from cultural expressions and historical artifacts to provide evidence for God's truth. Cultural apologetics contends that no narrative other than the biblical metanarrative can make comprehensive sense of the aspirations and achievements that enrich our lives with glimmers of truth, beauty, and goodness.[20]

---

20. Joshua Chatraw rightly notes that, in one sense, "all apologetics is cultural apologetics" because "persuasion always happens within a particular culture," Joshua Chatraw

Imaginative apologetics is a type of cultural apologetics that involves analyzing art, music, and literature to show how every positive ideal in these cultural expressions points to the desirability and coherence of the Christian worldview.[21] The imaginative apologist is likely to resonate with Kurt Vonnegut's concession that "the only proof he ever needed of the existence of God was music."[22] Narrative apologetics—as practiced, for example, by Alister McGrath and Joshua Chatraw—is yet another type of cultural apologetics, with a focus on showing how the Christian narrative tells a better story than any alternative.[23] Much of Francis Schaeffer's engagement with the arts fits well within the category of cultural apologetics.

Worldview Apologetics

Worldview apologetics is an approach connected closely to cultural and presuppositional apologetics. Worldview apologists identify and compare the worldviews that sustain different religious, political, and cultural commitments with the goal of demonstrating defective patterns in non-Christian ways of thinking. This process requires analyses of historical artifacts, cultural creations, competing epistemological commitments, and political policies—which means that worldview apologists apply both cultural and presuppositional tools to craft their case for Christian faith. Since worldview apologetics includes components of cultural and presuppositional apologetics, I've identified this approach on the map as a pathway that connects the cultural and presuppositional regions.[24]

---

and Mark Allen, *The Augustine Way: Retrieving a Vision for the Church's Apologetic Witness* (Baker, 2023), 14. However, "cultural apologetics," as used in this book, is focused not on *culture as the context* of apologetics but on *culture as epistemology-shaping social framework* exhibited through cultural expressions, artifacts, and narratives.

21. For a summary of the need for imaginative apologetics in a secular age, see John Hughes, "Proofs and Arguments," in *Imaginative Apologetics: Theology, Philosophy and the Catholic Tradition*, ed. Andrew Davison (SCM, 2011), 7–11. See also Holly Ordway, *Apologetics and the Christian Imagination: An Integrated Approach to Defending the Faith* (Emmaus Road, 2017).

22. Kurt Vonnegut, "Knowing What's Nice," *In These Times*, November 6, 2003, https://inthesetimes.com/article/knowing-whats-nice.

23. Joshua Chatraw, *Telling a Better Story: How to Talk About God in a Skeptical Age* (Zondervan, 2020), 7–13; Alister McGrath, *Narrative Apologetics: Sharing the Relevance, Joy, and Wonder of the Christian Tradition* (Baker, 2019), 98–100.

24. For an example of how worldview apologetics can bring together presuppositional and cultural apologetics, see James N. Anderson, *What's Your Worldview? An Interactive Approach to Life's Big Questions* (Crossway, 2014).

The Border That Isn't Typically Crossed

Most of the borders on the map of apologetics methods are dotted lines because different apologetics methods can and frequently do draw from one another. One boundary on the map is drawn as a solid line, however, and that's the borderline between classical apologetics and presuppositional apologetics. Apologists typically don't move back and forth across the boundary between presuppositional apologetics and classical apologetics. That's because these two perspectives start with very different sets of assumptions about how to defend the truth of Christianity. The classical apologist sees belief in the existence of a deity as a step in the direction of Christianity and is convinced that this belief can be proven based on arguments from nature and reason. The presuppositionalist contends that no neutral common ground exists between the Christian and the non-Christian from which to make a rational case for theism, so the apologist should focus instead on unmasking the irrationality of the non-Christian's resistance to God's existence.[25]

What About Other Apologetics Positions?

As you study my map of apologetics methods, you'll notice four positions along the edges of the circle. You might think of these four subsidiary practices—Reformed epistemology,[26] cumulative-case apologetics,[27]

---

25. This is not to suggest that presuppositional arguments can be utilized only by presuppositionalists or that only classical apologists can deploy classical arguments. A classical or evidential apologist could incorporate presuppositional reasoning to clear away points at which a non-Christian's pre-theoretical commitments prevent receptivity to cogent evidence. Presuppositional apologists might capitalize on classical arguments to unmask the irrationality of godless worldviews. However, in both cases, the function of the arguments becomes fundamentally different when utilized in the context of a different apologetics method. See Cornelius Van Til, *The Defense of the Faith*, ed. K. Scott Oliphint, 4th ed. (P&R, 2008), 28–29, 255–57.

26. Reformed epistemology is positioned between classical apologetics and presuppositional apologetics because this position, like classical apologetics, employs a form of foundationalism and, like presuppositionalism, emphasizes a universal *sensus divinitatis* and rejects the notion of neutral common ground. See Kelly James Clark, "Reformed Epistemology Apologetics," *Five Views*, 277–78, 282.

27. Cumulative-case apologetics is positioned between classical apologetics and evidential apologetics because this approach utilizes both classical and evidential arguments to form its inference to the best explanation. See Paul Feinberg, "Cumulative Case Apologetics," *Five Views*, 160–65; and Gary Habermas, "Cumulative Case Apologetics: An Evidentialist's Response," *Five Views*, 184–86.

EPISTEMOLOGY
(from Greek *epistēmē*, knowledge)
Study of the nature, origins, and limits of human knowledge.

verificational apologetics,[28] and ecclesial apologetics[29]—like outposts or ports that are dependent on resources from the primary apologetics methods on the mainland. Or maybe you could envision these practices as supplementary spinoffs tied to the primary apologetics methods in much the same way that J. R. R. Tolkien's *The Lord of the Rings* links to the more comprehensive world of *The Silmarillion* or *The Clone Wars* animated series connects to the *Star Wars* feature films. Spinoffs and supplements are incomplete by themselves, but each partial story strengthens and enriches the larger story.

Regardless of whether you think about the four subsidiary practices as outposts or spinoffs or something else altogether, none of these practices can construct a complete case for the truth of Christianity by itself. Each one borrows evidences and philosophical concepts from other approaches. Yet each of these practices can supplement the primary methods in ways that strengthen and enrich the case for Christian faith.

Since these are subsidiary positions, *Understanding Apologetics* doesn't include chapters on each one, but it's important for you to be aware of these positions since they are mentioned from time to time in the book. Due to the recent resurgence of interest in theological retrieval, I have included

---

28. Verificational apologetics is positioned between evidential apologetics and cultural apologetics because this approach presupposes a Christian worldview while utilizing historical evidences as one aspect of verifying the hypothesis of Christianity. "Verificational" is not used here in the logical positivist sense in which a statement remains a hypothesis unless it is proven true either by analysis of the statement itself or by empirical observations. "Verificational," in this context, describes an approach in which historical evidences are recognized as verifications and explanations of propositional revelation. See Bryan Follis, *Truth with Love: The Apologetics of Francis Schaeffer* (Crossway, 2006), 99–122; Carl F. H. Henry, *God, Revelation and Authority*, vol. 1 (Crossway, 1999), 245–72; Gordon Lewis, "Schaeffer's Apologetic Method," in *Reflections on Francis Schaeffer*, ed. Ronald Ruegsegger (Zondervan, 1986), 69–104; John Pearcey, "Yes and No: Carl F. H. Henry and the Question of Empirical Verification" (MPhil thesis, Institute for Christian Studies, 1987); Francis Schaeffer, *The God Who Is There*, in *The Francis A. Schaeffer Trilogy* (Crossway, 1990), 53–65; and James Orr, *The Christian View of God and the World* (Regents Park, 2001), 63–78.

29. Ecclesial apologetics is positioned between presuppositional apologetics and cultural apologetics because this approach, like presuppositionalism, appeals to transcendental arguments and yet, similar to cultural apologetics, seeks to show how divine truth fulfills and subverts the ideals of the prevalent culture, albeit with a positive focus on the church instead of an analytical focus on cultural expressions and artifacts. For an example of overlap between cultural apologetics and ecclesial apologetics, see Christopher Watkin, *Biblical Critical Theory: How the Bible's Unfolding Story Makes Sense of Modern Life and Culture* (Zondervan, 2022), 469–76.

a chapter on ecclesial apologetics to demonstrate how an ancient apologetics practice might be retrieved and recontextualized today.[30] Ecclesial apologetics was one of the key approaches to apologetics in the second and third centuries AD, and several recent scholars have pointed out parallels between contemporary Western culture and the cultures of the second century.[31] These parallels provide an opportunity for us to consider how ancient and medieval apologetics methods might be modified and applied in contemporary contexts.

The Four Subsidiary Practices

REFORMED EPISTEMOLOGY

Position holding that belief in the person of God may be rationally held as a basic belief in response to a sense of God's presence, with or without evidence. Beliefs may be properly basic as long as the person holding the beliefs has cognitive faculties that are (1) functioning properly, (2) aimed at truth, and (3) reliable in the environments for which they were designed. Every person's cognitive mechanisms include an awareness of the divine (*sensus divinitatis*), a belief-forming faculty similar to perception, memory, and introspection. Although unable to make a complete case for the truth of Christianity, Reformed epistemology can clear away objections related to the rationality of Christian belief. Reformed epistemology is a philosophical position that engages with foundationalism and basic beliefs, much like classical apologetics. At the same time, similar to presuppositionalism, Reformed epistemology suggests that everyone is designed with an awareness of the divine and there is no belief-neutral foundation from which to argue for God's existence. Proponents include Alvin Plantinga, Nicholas Wolterstorff, and Kelly James Clark.

CUMULATIVE-CASE APOLOGETICS

Position which argues for the truth of Christianity by demonstrating that Christianity provides a better explanation of reality than any

---

30. For the rise of evangelical interest in theological retrieval, see Gavin Ortlund, *Theological Retrieval for Evangelicals: Why We Need Our Past to Have a Future* (Crossway, 2019), 17–28.

31. See, e.g., Michael Kruger, *Christianity at the Crossroads: How the Second Century Shaped the Future of the Church* (InterVarsity, 2018), 230. See also Gerald Sittser, *Resilient Faith: How the Early Christian Third Way Changed the World* (Brazos, 2019), 15; and Trueman, *The Rise and Triumph of the Modern Self*, 454.

alternative when all available evidence is considered. Using the same facts and similar arguments as classical and evidential apologists, cumulative-case apologists test whether Christianity and its alternatives are noncontradictory, commensurate with reality, livable, and comprehensive and simple in their explanations. Many types of evidence may be included to establish truth with clear and convincing certainty, much like case evidence gathered in a courtroom. Proponents include Richard Swinburne, Douglas Groothuis, and J. Warner Wallace.

Verificational Apologetics

Position which presupposes Christianity and verifies the hypothesis of Christianity by testing it for internal consistency with itself, external consistency with evidence, and livability. Historical, cultural, and creational evidences do not establish the truth of Scripture, but they are able to verify the propositions of revelation found in the self-attesting and self-authenticating Scriptures. Verificational apologetics can look very similar to evidential or cumulative-case apologetics in practice, although the underlying assumptions of each approach are different. Proponents have included E. J. Carnell, Gordon Lewis, and Francis Schaeffer.

Ecclesial Apologetics

Ancient practice that points to the truth of Christianity as the best explanation for the existence and the ethics of the church. The moral framework enacted through the life of the church is impossible apart from the power of Christ and the truth of the biblical metanarrative. Much like cultural apologists, ecclesial apologists seek to show how the church's ethics and metanarrative provide a better story for people's lives and a better explanation for cultural truth, beauty, and goodness than any alternative. Ancient practitioners of this approach included Aristides, Athenagoras, and the author of the *Epistle to Diognetus*.

Mark Your Method with Meekness

I'm excited about what you'll learn in the pages that follow, but I must admit that I'm also a little bit concerned. Why does it concern me that you're learning different methods of apologetics? It's partly because well-intended Christians can become so passionate about a particular apologetics method that they forget its purpose. When that happens, apologists may expend more energy trying to convince other Christians to accept their preferred method than they do sharing the gospel with non-Christians.

My concern is also because of a troubling trend I've recently noticed. Cultural shifts have turned every Christian into an apologist. In response, there are those who suggest that the current cultural moment necessitates engaging secular people with sarcasm and snark, harshness and mockery. When that happens, the timbre of our ecclesial and moral speech becomes indistinguishable from the vitriol of current political discourse.

Some church leaders justify this rhetorical shift by appealing to Old Testament examples, apparently believing that our ecclesial discourse should function as the verbal equivalent of Samuel hacking Agag into pieces or Elijah mocking the priests of Baal before slaughtering them (1 Sam 15:32–33; 1 Kgs 18:27–40). We, however, live within the new covenant, and we are the recipients of a Spirit whose fruit includes peace and patience, gentleness and kindness (Eph 5:22–23). Because we are secure in this Spirit, every word spoken to those outside the faith should be rich with grace (Col 4:6). Still others rationalize their rhetoric by claiming the example of Jesus flipping tables in the temple or condemning the religious leaders (Matt 23:13–36). And yet, as Daniel Darling has pointed out, "We are not Jesus, given a divine mandate by the Father to cleanse and purify God's house. And while we know Jesus's motives when angry were always justified, we can't be as sure about our own."[32]

Every non-Christian—even the one who despises and opposes what we believe—is an embodied image of God and a potential heir of God's kingdom, broken by sin and yet unspeakably precious and beautiful. "There are," C. S. Lewis once declared, "no ordinary people. You have never talked to a mere mortal. Nations, cultures, arts, civilizations—these are mortal, and their life is to ours as the life of a gnat. But it is immortals whom we joke with, work with, marry, snub, and exploit."[33] Simon Peter understood this truth well. When he penned a letter to socially marginalized Christians living on the cusp of persecution, Peter urged his readers to engage their interlocutors with "gentleness and reverence" (1 Pet 3:15–16).[34] Despite writing

32. Daniel Darling, *Agents of Grace: How to Bridge Divides and Love as Jesus Loved* (Zondervan, 2023), 123.

33. C. S. Lewis, "The Weight of Glory," in *The Weight of Glory* (HarperOne, 2001), 46.

34. First Peter seems to have been written between the AD 41 expulsion of Jewish persons, including Jewish Christians, from Rome and the persecution of Christians that began in the aftermath of the fire in Rome in AD 64. See Karen Jobes, *1 Peter* (Baker, 2005), 37–41. The recipients of the letter were facing intense social pressure that included exclusion and social ostracism (43, 45).

to Christians in a far more negative world than any contemporary condition of secularity has concocted, his call was for them to conduct themselves in ways marked by meekness and holiness (1:14–15; 3:15–16). Meekness of this sort shouldn't be confused with weakness, but it certainly can't coexist in the church's rhetorical toolbox alongside snark or rage.[35] Sarcastic social media posts may shame our detractors for a few passing moments and provide us with a fleeting sense of superiority, but such ungodly behavior does not direct anyone to the gospel.

According to Peter, God works through meekness and fear coupled with holy conduct to produce godly shame in the lives of our persecutors (3:16). If these persecutors do not repent and receive the gospel, then their eternal shame at the end of time will serve as the vindication of our meekness (2:6–8). It is precisely because we are confident in the eschatological shame of those who defy our Lord and his Christ that we can imitate the example of Jesus here and now, even in a negative world: "When he was insulted, he did not insult in return" (2:23).

If we engage non-Christians with mockery instead of meekness or insults instead of gentleness, our words may defend God's truth, but our works defy God's truth. As Keith Plummer has noted, "Treating either non-Christians or fellow believers with derision, contempt, and incivility is exactly the opposite of what we are commanded concerning adorning the teaching of our great God and Savior (Titus 2:10)."[36] And so, no matter what apologetics method you choose, choose meekness alongside your method and fall more in love with the gospel than you do with any method.

We are all apologists now. The question is not whether you will do apologetics; the only question is how. Regardless of how you choose to do apologetics, may your methods be marked by meekness. If your apologetics method isn't meek, it isn't biblical, no matter how biblical the content you teach may be.

---

35. For Aristotle, "gentleness" or "meekness" (πραΰντικά) was the opposite of being enraged. See Aristotle, "Τέχνης Ρητορικής," 1380a.10–11. "Reverence" or "fear" (φόβου) in 1 Peter 3:15–16 could describe either fear of God or respect toward interlocutors. For fear of God as the sense of this text, see Paul Achtemeier, *1 Peter* (Fortress, 1996), 234. "Meekness" and "fear," however, also occur in close proximity in Aristotle's Τέχνης Ρητορικής, with both terms referring to the speaker's disposition toward hearers. This pattern might favor interpreting "fear" in 1 Peter as respect for the persons to whom Christians give a defense, although it is also possible that the recipients of Peter's letter were meant to consider that God himself would be listening to their defense.

36. Keith Plummer, "The World Is Watching," in *The Digital Public Square: Christian Ethics in a Technological Society*, ed. Jason Thacker (B&H, 2023), 340.

Resources for Further Reading About Apologetics Methods

Cowan, Steven, ed. *Five Views on Apologetics*. Zondervan, 2000.

Forrest, Benjamin, Joshua Chatraw, and Alister McGrath. *The History of Apologetics: A Biographical and Methodological Introduction*. Zondervan, 2020.

Guinness, Os. *Fool's Talk: Recovering the Art of Christian Persuasion*. InterVarsity, 2019.

Kreeft, Peter, and Ronald Tacelli. *Handbook of Christian Apologetics*. Reprint edition. InterVarsity, 1994.

Morley, Brian. *Mapping Apologetics: Comparing Contemporary Approaches*. InterVarsity, 2015.

Sweis, Khaldoun, and Chad Meister, eds. *Christian Apologetics: An Anthology of Primary Sources*. Zondervan, 2024.

1

Classical Apologetics

Melissa Cain Travis

In his spiritual autobiography *Surprised by Joy*, C. S. Lewis recounts his lengthy, complex, and angst-ridden journey to faith. While orthodox Christianity was his eventual destination, he assented—with a great deal of reluctance—to mere theism quite some time before his philosophical and theological wanderings culminated in his conversion. Lewis describes both rational and arational influences—those that engaged his keen philosophical mind as well as those that affected him on an imaginative or visceral level—that served as a series of stepping-stones leading him to the fullness of the Christian faith. While he was a preparatory school student, it was Norse mythology that unexpectedly reawakened his longing for an inscrutable "Other."[1] Years later, it was George MacDonald's faerie story *Phantastes* that baptized his imagination (as he puts it) and set it at odds with his rationalistic unbelief. The essays of Christian writer G. K. Chesterton, which he discovered while serving in the Great War, were another significant factor.[2] At Oxford University, his study of philosophy convinced him of what he called "the Absolute," and the literary art of the Western tradition further stoked his insatiable yearning for "Joy itself." The final phase of his odyssey included an intensive study of the major world religions and the historical

1. C. S. Lewis, *Surprised by Joy: The Shape of My Early Life* (Houghton Mifflin Harcourt, 2012), 73.

2. Lewis, *Surprised by Joy*, 191. Lewis remarks, "In reading Chesterton, as in reading MacDonald, I did not know what I was letting myself in for. A young man who wishes to remain a sound Atheist cannot be too careful of his reading."

Jesus of Nazareth, whom Lewis regarded as the actuality of the Other, the fulfillment of Joy, the Myth that became Fact.[3]

Many others have described similarly complex journeys involving a diversity of evidence, arguments, and experiences that contributed to their conversions.[4] Some began to doubt materialism when they encountered scientific information that supported the idea of a designing intelligence behind the universe. Others were troubled by the lack of justification for their deep-seated convictions about morality and human significance. Some sensed intimations of the transcendent in works of great literature or film, or they experienced sublimity in nature that moved them to consider spiritual explanations for the human response to overwhelming beauty. The conclusion that seems to follow naturally from these real-world data is that the Holy Spirit uniquely tailors God's approach to each individual, engaging different aspects of the soul.

As co-laborers in the building of God's kingdom, we have the incredible honor of participating in this project of eternal significance. It is a project we must approach with the understanding that there is no one-size-fits-all protocol for effective engagement with a nonbeliever. A conversation about Christianity will proceed quite differently with an entrenched materialist compared to someone who is at least somewhat open to supernaturalism or who embraces some sort of theism yet harbors reservations about Christian doctrine. Those who are largely apathetic toward spiritual questions need to have their latent desire for the transcendent awakened prior to being engaged in philosophical and theological discussion regarding what (or Who) can fully satisfy that desire.[5] The most appropriate apologetic technique in any given instance depends on a myriad of contextual and personal factors, and our apologetics must have the plasticity to adapt accordingly.

---

3. Lewis elaborated on this description of the incarnation in his 1944 essay "Myth Became Fact." See C. S. Lewis, *God in the Dock*, ed. Walter Hooper (Eerdmans, 1970), 58–60.

4. Lee Strobel is one of the more widely known, but there have been many others. See Lee Strobel, *The Case for Christ: A Journalist's Personal Investigation of the Evidence for Jesus* (Zondervan, 1998).

5. As Paul Gould has defined it, cultural apologetics is "the work of establishing the Christian voice, conscience, and imagination within a culture so that Christianity is seen as true and satisfying." Gould envisions this project as one that encompasses and integrates the rational, imaginative, and moral categories of apologetics. Cultural apologetics as Gould defines it overlaps significantly with the vision of holistic classical apologetics I articulate in this chapter. See Paul Gould, *Cultural Apologetics* (Zondervan, 2019), 21.

A Definition of Classical Apologetics

Classical apologetics is a two-step approach to apologetics that appeals to a variety of sources to establish the plausibility of God's existence and then defends Christian doctrines based on historical and other evidences.[6] It proceeds on the fundamental assumption that common grace is granted to all image-bearers by the Holy Spirit, enabling them to thoughtfully consider matters related to God and Christianity. The classical apologist believes human beings have shared understandings of some aspects of reality that allow us to find islands of common ground upon which to initiate such conversations. Otherwise, evangelistic apologetics would be impossible.

CLASSICAL APOLOGETICS

Two-step apologetics method that (1) appeals to reason and nature to establish the plausibility of God's existence and then (2) defends Christian doctrines based on historical and cultural evidences.

HOLISTIC CLASSICAL APOLOGETICS

Approach to classical apologetics that seeks to make a case for God's existence by engaging the intellect, imagination, aesthetic sensibilities, and innate existential longings, and then to use philosophical, historical, and cultural elements to show the truth of the gospel and the inherent goodness of Christianity.

Ideally, the classical apologetics strategy will be integrative and holistic, engaging the different aspects of the human person: the intellect, imagination, conscience, aesthetic sensibilities, and innate existential longings. Often, as Blaise Pascal understood, we need first to make Christianity desirable to nonbelievers by helping them see its unrivaled goodness and beauty before attempting to show that it is indeed *true*.[7] In common parlance, we engage the heart to open the mind. Perhaps an appropriate term for this perspective is *holistic* classical apologetics.

Holistic classical apologetics acknowledges the continual guiding role of the Holy Spirit in a person's journey to faith. At the same time, it emphasizes the value of recognizing the philosophical, evidential, and cultural factors that have played a role in conversions to Christianity. If anything should influence our approach to apologetics, it should be these documented realities that teach us about the Holy Spirit's pursuit of God's unique, image-bearing

6. This methodology is resonant with the classical "two books" philosophy of divine revelation, which boasts a rich intellectual pedigree within historical, orthodox Christianity, one that can be traced all the way back to the ante-Nicene fathers. In this view, natural revelation may serve to illuminate the meaning of Scripture and vice versa.

7. Blaise Pascal, *Pensées*, trans. Roger Ariew (Hackett, 2004), 9 (S46/L12).

creatures. Apologists cooperate with the Spirit by preparing themselves to be used in the Spirit's work at every opportunity, not only for the good of other souls but also for their own sanctification.

A Biblical and Historical Defense of Classical Apologetics

A defense of classical methodology necessarily entails making a case for the validity of natural theology as part of the apologetics project. This case may be made from a historical, philosophical, or theological perspective (or some combination thereof). The historical approach is concerned with demonstrating the longstanding position of the church on natural revelation by surveying the work of influential theologians and philosophers. To that end, what follows is a chronological examination that begins with patristic literature and proceeds through a selection of writings from key figures of subsequent eras.

My objective is to show that the universal accessibility of natural revelation, based on passages such as Romans 1:20, has been widely assumed throughout Christian history.[8] This defense will culminate with historical evidence of a different sort: the accounts of contemporary adult converts. These accounts, like C. S. Lewis's, will support classical apologetics by providing evidence for theism preceding and leading to Christian conversion in some cases as well as for the multidimensional nature of the spiritual journey, which justifies a definitively holistic classical vision for apologetic engagement.

---

8. A thorough exposition of such passages is beyond the scope of this chapter, but a concise defense of the traditional interpretation of Paul's statement in Romans (since it is the most relevant for present purposes) may be helpful. In his commentary on the epistle, Douglas Moo offers the following: "But just what does Paul mean when he claims that human beings 'see' and 'understand' from creation and history that a powerful God exists? Some think that Paul is asserting only that people have around them the evidence of God's existence and basic qualities; whether people actually perceive it or become personally conscious of it is not clear. Yet Paul's wording suggests more than this. He asserts that people actually come to 'understand' something about God's existence and nature. How universal is this perception? The flow of Paul's argument makes any limitation impossible. Those who perceive the attributes of God in creation must be the same as those who suppress the truth in unrighteousness and are therefore liable to the wrath of God. Paul makes clear that this includes all people (see 3:9, 19–20)." Douglas Moo, *The Epistle to the Romans*, 2nd ed. (Eerdmans, 2018), 116. As the historical data will show, Moo's view reflects a traditional understanding of natural revelation.

Natural Theology Among Ancient and Medieval Christians

Second-century apologist Justin Martyr was educated in various pagan philosophies prior to his adult conversion to Christianity. His desire to know God was the primary reason he pursued his studies, yet these studies left him dissatisfied.[9] In his *Exhortation to the Greeks*, Justin first acknowledges that the writings of various prominent pagan poets and philosophers reflect an affirmation, based on natural revelation, of one eternal God. Yet, he says, this foundational knowledge is gravely insufficient and syncretized with all manner of pagan error. To reach "true religion," the Greeks must take the essential next step of examining the historical and prophetic evidence for Christianity.[10]

In his *First Apology*, Justin specifically mentions Socrates as one who had reasoned to the truth of monotheism and was sentenced to death because of this teaching. Socrates's conclusion resulted from the prevailing influence of "reason . . . the Logos himself, who assumed a human form and became man, and was called Jesus Christ."[11] (*Logos* is the Greek term for "word" or "reason." In the writings of the Greek philosophers, *logos* described the universal divine reason that was immanent in nature and yet transcended the imperfections of the cosmos.) The implicit assertion here

9. Justin Martyr, *Dialogue with Trypho*, 2, in *The First Apology, The Second Apology, Dialogue with Trypho, Exhortation to the Greeks, Discourse to the Greeks, The Monarchy of the Rule of God*, trans. Thomas Falls (Catholic University of America Press, 2008).

10. He writes, "Now is the hour, O Greeks, that you (convinced by your own historians that Moses and the other Prophets were far more ancient than any of those whom you honored as sages among you) renounce the ancient error of your ancestors and read the sacred prophetic writings in order to learn from them the true religion. The Prophets do not strive to impress you with a skillful use of words, nor do they resort to specious or persuasive arguments (a device of those who endeavor to rob you of the truth), but with the simple words and phrases that first come to mind they relate to you whatever the Holy Spirit, who descended upon them, wished to transmit through them to those desirous of knowing the true religion. Renounce, therefore, all human respect, and the time-worn error of mankind, and the empty sound of pompous passages (through the use of which you consider yourselves possessed of every advantage), and devote yourselves to truly profitable things. It cannot be said that you will offend your ancestors by embracing a doctrine opposed to their error, since they very probably are now bewailing their lot in Hades and are touched with deep remorse and repentance. Were it possible for them to warn you of what happened to them after their death, you would surely know from what terrible evils they wished you to be saved." Justin Martyr, *Exhortation to the Greeks*, 35.

11. Justin Martyr, *First Apology*, 5.

is that human beings, with their God-given rational faculties, unwittingly participate in the *Logos*—the paradigm of reason—through the exercise of those faculties and may thereby arrive at the necessary truth of God's existence. Justin's apologetic affirms that special revelation found in Scripture is indispensable for sufficient knowledge of divine truth.

Athanasius of Alexandria, a Greek father of the church widely recognized for his defense of Nicene theology, often cited the order and harmony of nature as evidence for God. In *Against the Heathen*, he writes that it is "possible to attain to the knowledge of God from the things which are seen, since Creation, as though in written characters, declares in a loud voice, by its order and harmony, its own Lord and Creator."[12] Here he draws a parallel between the Word, or *Logos*, by whom all things were made (John 1:1–3) and the words of human language.[13] In other words, just as we can rightfully attribute instances of spoken or written words to rational minds, so we can regard the order and artistic splendor of nature as indicative of a transcendent Maker and the divine *Logos*. Athanasius celebrates the grand cosmic harmony in which the observable orderliness of creation manifests the mind that designed it:

> Since . . . there is everywhere not disorder but order, proportion and not disproportion, not disarray but arrangement, and that in an order perfectly harmonious, we must infer and be led to perceive the harmony in them. For though He be not seen with the eyes, yet from the order and harmony of things contrary it is possible to perceive their Ruler, Arranger, and King.[14]

Athanasius then proceeds to argue that the intricacy and diversity of created things existing in marvelous harmony are indicative of a single Creator God rather than many gods.

---

12. Athanasius, *On the Incarnation* with *Against the Heathen* (Paterikon, 2018), 63.

13. After quoting from Wisdom of Solomon 13:5— "By the greatness and the beauty of the creatures proportionately the Maker of them is seen"—he writes: "For just as by looking up to the heaven and seeing its order and the light of the stars, it is possible to infer the Word Who ordered these things, so by beholding the Word of God, one needs must behold also God His Father, proceeding from Whom He is rightly called His Father's Interpreter and Messenger. And this one may see from our own experience; for if when a word proceeds from men we infer that the mind is its source, and by thinking about the word, see with our reason the mind which it reveals, by far greater evidence and incomparably more, seeing the power of the Word, we receive knowledge also of His good Father." See Athanasius, *On the Incarnation*, 77–79.

14. Athanasius, *On the Incarnation*, 69.

The idea that creation points to a divine mind in a manner analogous to the ways that written language or harmonious music are evidence of a human mind serves as a precursor to the "book of nature" metaphor found in the works of Augustine of Hippo. Augustine was one of the most influential theologians of the Western Christian tradition. In one of his sermons, he gives what is possibly the earliest explicit statement of this metaphor:

> Some read a book to find God. But there is a great book: the spectacle of what has been created. Look upwards and downward; pay attention and read. In order to enable you to read that book, God did not write in letters with ink but he placed what is created itself in front of you. Why do you seek a louder voice? Heaven and earth are crying to you: God made me.[15]

Augustine does not believe the Creator could be any more obvious than he already is in his natural revelation of himself. The book of nature (*liber naturae*) is, unlike the text of Scripture, accessible to the illiterate, so all can attain some knowledge of God. Augustine explains that the mind of humankind, by virtue of humanity's creation in God's image, is divinely illuminated in a way that enables perception of the rationality that pervades nature.[16]

In his *Confessions*, Augustine affirms the concept of natural revelation in both the rational and aesthetic sense. As the work of a rational creator and supreme artist, God's creation exhibits both intellectual and sensible beauty. Augustine paraphrases Romans 1:20 in reference to his own thinking: "I was absolutely sure that since the founding of the universe, the unseen things that belong to you have been seen and comprehended through the things that are made, and your eternal power and divinity are seen and comprehended along with them."[17] Later, in one of the most intensely poetic passages of this spiritual memoir, he explains how the aesthetic and rational attributes of creation proclaim a divine Maker rather than some kind of intrinsic divinity:

---

15. Augustine, *Sermons: 51–94* (New City Press, 1991), 225–26.

16. Augustine, *Eighty-three Different Questions* (Catholic University of America Press, 2010), 248. In his lectures on the Gospel of John, Augustine argues in a similar vein: "For such is the energy of the true Godhead, that it cannot be altogether and utterly hidden from any rational creature, so long as it makes use of its reason. . . . In respect, therefore, of His being the maker of this world that is visible in heaven and earth around us, God was known unto all nations even before they were indoctrinated into the faith of Christ." Augustine, *On the Gospel of John*, as quoted in David Haines, *Natural Theology: A Biblical and Historical Introduction and Defense* (Davenant, 2024), 115.

17. Augustine, *Confessions*, trans. Sarah Ruden (Random House, 2017), 7.23.

> But what is it that I love? I asked the earth, and it said, "It's not me," and everything in it admitted the same thing. I asked the sea and the great chasms of the deep, and the creeping things that have the breath of life in them, and they answered, "We aren't your God: search above us." I asked the gusty winds, and all the atmosphere there is, along with its inhabitants. . . . I asked the sky, the sun, the moon, the stars, and they said, "We're not the God you're looking for, either." I told all those beings who stand around outside my body's gates, its senses, "Tell me about my God. You aren't him, but tell me something about him." And they declared with a shout, "He made us!" My question was the act of focusing on them, and their response was their beauty.[18]

It should be noted that Augustine did not believe the knowledge offered by natural revelation was impossible to deny. Instead, he laments that many are so taken with created things themselves that they do not discern the higher truth.

> It's not as if the objects alter what they say—their beauty, that is—between the person who merely observes them and the other who observes and questions. . . . No, actually, it speaks to everyone, but it's only understood by those who compare with the truth inside themselves the voice taken in from outside themselves. It's the truth that tells me, "Your God isn't the earth and sky, or any material thing." The very nature of material things says this.[19]

For Augustine, God's natural revelation involves more than the attributes of the external world and our corresponding rational and aesthetic capacities. In his moving opening passage of the *Confessions*, he makes a statement that might be regarded as a precursor to the Lewisian argument from desire.[20] He cites the incessant undercurrent of longing with which we move through life that cannot be fulfilled by earthly things: "In yourself you rouse us, giving us delight in glorifying you, because you made us with yourself as our goal, and our heart is restless until it rests in you."[21] The remainder of the work is Augustine's lengthy prayer of confession for the futile ways that he attempted to assuage this longing before surrendering his life to Christ. His words suggest that he understands this phenomenon of the inner life as evidence of our proper end: communion with our Maker.

---

18. Augustine, *Confessions*, 10.9.
19. Augustine, *Confessions*, 10.10.
20. "If I find in myself a desire which no experience in this world can satisfy, the most probable explanation is that I was made for another world." C. S. Lewis, *Mere Christianity* (HarperCollins, 2000), 136–37.
21. Augustine, *Confessions*, 1.1.

Thomas Aquinas was a premier theologian and philosopher of the high Middle Ages whose influence regarding classical apologetics is difficult to overstate. Aquinas argues that there are necessary preambles to the faith—such as the existence of God—that can be demonstrated by the light of natural reason, without any appeal to the special revelation of Scripture.[22] The truths of sacred Scripture are both necessary and sufficient for salvation, according to Aquinas, but the knowledge of God's existence is available to all, though not universally obtained for various reasons.[23] Some knowledge of God is thus twofold: It is gleaned from natural revelation as well as special revelation. Yet, there are truths that only Scripture provides, such as the Trinity and the gospel. This is resonant with the "two books" idea that had, by the time of Aquinas, been part of the Christian intellectual tradition for many centuries.

Thomas Aquinas repeatedly cites the apostle Paul's words in Romans 1:20 as a supremely authoritative affirmation of the universal accessibility of natural revelation. As philosopher and theologian David Haines puts it: "Aquinas suggests that this verse would be false if we could not naturally know that God is. God does not lie, and His Word is always true. Therefore, it is possible to naturally know the truth of the statement, 'God is.'"[24] Aquinas's "Five Ways" that this proposition can be demonstrated, which draw from a long and rich philosophical tradition, are the most widely known demonstrations of this truth.[25] He does not suggest that a comprehensive definition of God can be ascertained through these five ways, only that each of the ways infers the being we refer to as "God." He specifies that this knowledge of God is not sufficient for salvation but is logically prior to belief in the truth of Christianity.

---

22. Philosopher and theologian David Haines helpfully articulates Aquinas's position in this way: "The preambles to faith are affirmed and assumed by special revelation but are not proved by Sacred Theology. Rather, they are properly proved in philosophy and are accepted as true by the theologian." Haines, *Natural Theology*, 146.

23. For further discussion, see Haines, *Natural Theology*, 150–51.

24. Haines, *Natural Theology*, 175.

25. The five ways are (1) the necessity of an "unmoved mover" that is ultimately responsible for change (and prevents an infinite regress of "changers"); (2) the necessity of a first efficient cause that is itself uncaused (and prevents an infinite regress of efficient causes); (3) the necessity of a necessarily existing cause of all contingent beings; (4) the demonstration that the first unmoved mover is the perfection of those things that are observed in gradations—goodness, truth, nobility—and the ground of being itself; and (5) the demonstration, based on teleology (end-directedness) in nature, of the existence of an intelligent, volitional creator who directs observable things to their proper ends. See Haines, *Natural Theology*, 186.

Natural Theology in the Reformation and Modern Eras

Philip Melancthon was a key intellectual leader in the German Reformation and an early Protestant systematic theologian as well as a close associate of Martin Luther. Melanchthon clearly saw nature as a mode of divine revelation. He championed logic and the mathematical arts—which included arithmetic, geometry, and astronomy—as essential aspects of theological training in Lutheran seminaries. He understood the fundamentally mathematical quality of the natural world as a material manifestation of divine rationality, and he saw the human aptitude for mathematical disciplines as that part of the image of God that allows humankind to apprehend God's natural revelation.[26] He argued that "vestiges of divinity" can be discerned in the heavens, traces of the mind of God in the orderly celestial motions.[27] Charlotte Methuen, a leading expert on the curriculum Melanchthon designed for the University of Tübingen, writes,

> Melanchthon explains that Paul in his letter to the Romans [1:20] encourages the study of philosophy in order that 'God's presence in nature' can be considered, for 'the whole of the universe is a sort of sacrament, because it is a testimony that God is, and that God is wise, good, just'. He points out that the human mind has been formed by God to study the heavens and to recognize the vestiges of divinity, but reminds his readers that the Word of God rules this philosophy, just as it does everything else. There is no mention of any special status for astronomy, although the movements of the heavenly bodies are specifically cited as evidence for God's existence.[28]

Melanchthon's idea was that the creation contains sensible manifestations of God's mind that are accessible to the human mind on account of its capacity to detect mathematical order and regularities. Through the discipline of astronomy, natural philosophers discovered "the manifest footprints of God in nature" and philosophers who rejected its practice were "deliberate atheists."[29] Had they studied astronomy, they would have "been forced to admit that this totality of things was both made and is governed

---

26. Rhonda Martens, *Kepler's Philosophy and the New Astronomy* (Princeton University Press, 2000), 12.

27. Charlotte Methuen, *Kepler's Tübingen: Stimulus to a Theological Mathematics* (Ashgate, 1998), 82.

28. Methuen, *Kepler's Tübingen*, 87.

29. Sachiko Kusukawa, *The Transformation of Natural Philosophy: The Case of Philip Melanchthon* (Cambridge University Press, 1995), 127.

by a certain Mind."[30] Melanchthon cites Genesis 1:14 as the biblical commendation of astronomical observation: "But if anybody asks for the authority from Scriptures which commends this study, he has the weightiest testimony in Genesis where it is written 'Let [the lights] be for signs and for seasons, and for days and years.'"[31] Melanchthon's work in revising the curriculum at Tübingen did much to shape the development of Lutheran theology and contributed to the natural philosophy that was integral to the Scientific Revolution.[32]

During the seventeenth and eighteenth centuries, as methodologies and instrumentation improved, knowledge about the natural world increased exponentially. Some renowned natural philosophers of this period were enthusiastic about the apologetic utility of natural revelation, and their writings and lectures were instrumental in the early modern proliferation of natural theology as a formal discipline.[33] Both atheism and deism were targeted

---

30. Kusukawa, *The Transformation of Natural Philosophy*, 127.

31. Kusukawa, *The Transformation of Natural Philosophy*, 127.

32. This occurred primarily through the monumental intellectual contributions of Johannes Kepler (1571–1630), whose motivations and achievements in astronomy—essential to the Scientific Revolution—were deeply rooted in the classical view of natural revelation, which influenced him immeasurably during his years at Tübingen and for the remainder of his life. His work functioned as the transformation of ancient astronomy into a mathematical celestial physics, a step that was essential to the rise of modern science. He thought of natural philosophers as performing a priestly duty: expositing God's book of nature, which allows us to gain a glimpse into the mind of our Creator—to "share in his own thoughts." Although he did not dedicate scholarly efforts to natural theology specifically, Kepler certainly believed that nature bears attributes that have positive implications for the existence of God, which even nonbelievers can recognize. In a letter that accompanied a copy of his *Mysterium Cosmographicum*, he writes: "Here is treated the Book of Nature which is so highly praised by the Holy Scriptures. Paul presents it to the heathens so that they may see God in it just as the sun can be observed in water or a mirror." Carola Baumgardt, *Johannes Kepler: Life and Letters* (Philosophical Library, 1951), 33, 50. Notice that Kepler's emphasis on the harmony of mathematics, rational minds, and the material world remains highly relevant to contemporary natural theology, specifically design arguments dealing with the applicability of mathematics to nature and the failure of materialism to account for human rationality. For further treatment of these topics, see Melissa Cain Travis, *Thinking God's Thoughts: Johannes Kepler and the Miracle of Cosmic Comprehensibility* (Roman Roads Press, 2022).

33. English chemist Robert Boyle (1627–1691), who is credited with the modern experimental method, is an outstanding example. A man of devout Christian faith, he was fascinated by the intricacies of living systems revealed by improved microscopes and the dynamics of the materials he could manipulate in his laboratory. He was passionate about celebrating the omniscience and foresight of the Creator by uncovering the interwoven complexities of nature that were revealed through his experiments, dissections, and microscopic observations. Moreover, he believed that nature is a legitimate source of theistic knowledge, and thought it was stupidity or perverseness to attribute the remarkable contrivances of

since the intricacies and harmonies of nature were considered evidence not only for a Creator but also for a Creator who is concerned with his creation. By the early nineteenth century, natural theology was experiencing what might be regarded as its golden age. Works such as William Paley's *Natural Theology* were broadly influential and mandatory reading at major universities such as Cambridge University, Paley's alma mater. Nearly three decades after the publication of Charles Darwin's *Origin of Species*, the prestigious Gifford Lectures were instituted at the four ancient universities in Scotland to promote and disseminate studies in natural theology. These lectures did not have to be denominationally specific or even exclusive to one religion; it was only required that "they treat their subject strictly as a natural science, the greatest of all possible sciences, indeed, in one sense the only science, that of Infinite Being, without reference to or reliance upon any supposed special exceptional or so-called miraculous revelation."[34]

After a period of decline that began in the early twentieth century,[35] natural theology experienced a renaissance thanks to the work of philosophers such as Richard Swinburne and William Lane Craig. Swinburne, Craig, and others have championed various philosophical arguments for the existence of God over the last several decades and have helped to revitalize Christian philosophy as well. The emergence of the formal Intelligent

---

nature to blind chance: "There are diverse things in the Book of the Creatures, in which there appear such manifest Impresses of Wisdom, that even according to the popular notions of men, and the superficial theories of vulgar Philosophers; 'tis obvious to conclude, that they [are] the effects of an Intelligent cause: and yet the same things upon a more attentive & skillful inspection, afford to a Philosophical Considerer of them, far greater or more convincing evidence of the power, wisdom & Beneficence of the Divine Author of things." J. J. MacIntosh, *Boyle on Atheism* (University of Toronto Press, 2005), 241. Upon his death, Boyle bequeathed an endowment for the institution of a lecture series on natural theology, the Boyle Lectures.

34. Stanley Jaki, *Lord Gifford and His Lectures* (Scottish Academic Press, 1986), 73–74.

35. The golden age of natural theology was not, as many have assumed, obliterated by the work of Charles Darwin. Although he certainly shaped thinking about natural theology in some quarters in a wide variety of ways, both positive and negative, the most significant factor in the decline of the discipline, especially in England, was the First World War. As Matthew Eddy writes, "It was very difficult for many people to see design in the face of the horrific atrocities that a moral God seemed to be allowing in such as devastating global war. . . . The inexplicable presence of such pervasive evil undermined the ways in which natural knowledge had been aligned with divine attributes like omniscience and omnipresence." This is not to say that natural theology disappeared altogether, or that Darwinian evolutionary theory was not viewed by some, particularly in the United States, as presenting a conflict with natural evidence for biblical creation, only that interest in this branch of theology seems to have waned considerably. See Matthew D. Eddy, "Nineteenth-Century Natural Theology," in *The Oxford Handbook of Natural Theology*, ed. Russell Re Manning, John Hedley Brook, and Fraser Watts (Oxford University Press, 2015), 114.

Design movement has further fueled renewed interest in the case for a cosmic and biological designer by elucidating certain attributes of nature that resist materialist explanation or from which intelligence may be rationally inferred. A quarter of the way into the twenty-first century, the discipline of natural theology seems to be enjoying unprecedented attention thanks to developments in analytic philosophy, increased support for the "God hypothesis" from the natural sciences, and technological advancements in mass communication.

This historical survey was intended to show that the traditional Christian view is that natural revelation is one way that knowledge of God's existence may be attained. To further support the legitimacy of holistic classical apologetics, I will now consider stories from converts who cite multiple kinds of evidence and experiences as important landmarks in their journey to faith through theism.

Classical Apologetics and Contemporary Conversion Accounts

In an essay titled "Is Theism Important?," C. S. Lewis remarks, "Nearly everyone I know who has embraced Christianity in adult life has been influenced by what seemed to him to be at least probable arguments for Theism."[36] Still today, testimonials indicate that conversions often proceed through an initial phase of theism and, like Lewis's, involve a variety of experiential and intellectual stepping-stones. The enormous value of conversion stories is that they illustrate the holistic, cumulative, and gradual nature of many journeys to faith, which is instructive for the Christian apologist. The two stories summarized below are paradigmatic in this respect.

Sy Garte is a biochemist, formerly of the National Institutes of Health, with more than two hundred scientific publications to his credit. He was raised by stridently atheist parents who were devoted to the anti-theist political philosophy of Marxism. As Garte explains, "My parents . . . laughed at the idea of God. They were sure that there was no God; there could be nothing like God. . . . My parents' atheism was indeed a deeply felt religious belief, and it was successfully transmitted to and accepted by me at a very young age."[37] As a young adult, Garte had the vague sense that there were

36. C. S. Lewis. "Is Theism Important?," *God in the Dock* (Eerdmans, 2014), 187.

37. Sy Garte, *The Works of His Hands: A Scientist's Journey from Atheism to Faith* (Kregel, 2019), 22.

logical inconsistencies between materialism and humanist ideals, but he remained content with social evolutionary explanations. While pursuing his scientific education and then during the early decades of his career, he began asking crucial questions about the world, such as whether all of reality is fully comprehensible through reason, how to ground human significance, and how the universe, the first life, and consciousness could have arisen through blind processes.

Deep down, Garte experienced the quintessential human longings for meaning and higher purpose, and he sought satisfaction in his professional endeavors.[38] Yet, as his scientific knowledge advanced, his philosophical questions multiplied. The first phenomenon he encountered that he considered a positive reason to believe in God was cosmic fine-tuning—the mathematical constants that must fall within extraordinarily narrow ranges in order for life or even chemistry itself to exist. Ultimately, it was the scientific problems presented by the origin of the universe, of life, and of consciousness that opened his mind to the real possibility of God's existence. Garte subsequently moved from atheism to agnosticism.

A church service Garte attended with a friend dispelled some key misconceptions he had always harbored about religion and the Christian message. The next lengthy phase of Garte's journey included intense dreams with themes of surrender and trust as the gateway to true security and joy. After attending church a few more times over several years, he came to understand the gospel message, but he was not yet willing to receive it. Finally, in 2006, as Garte drove alone along a Pennsylvania turnpike listening to the radio, a rhetorically talented preacher inspired him to imagine how he himself would present his hypothetical conversion story to an audience. During this mental exercise, he was emotionally overwhelmed by the thought of God's love for him. He recognizes now that this was the presence of the Holy Spirit and that many stepping-stones had prepared his mind and heart for that glorious moment. These stepping-stones included encounters with joy-inducing beauty, his recognition of the philosophical incoherence of materialist humanism and the theistic implications of scientific phenomena, the message of Christ's love and forgiveness, spiritually significant dreams,

38. Garte, 45, writes, "I found I simply could not accept anything on faith, since the whole concept of faith was missing in my worldview. As my scientific research career developed, I began to feel that it wasn't faith that I had been missing but the thing behind faith: the human need to believe in something, to find a system of thought, a way of seeing the world and everything in it that was comforting, sustaining, satisfying, and indeed joyous. I had found this in science, so science became my method for reaching spiritual goals."

and finally this direct encounter with the Holy Spirit.[39] Garte's experience was gradual, cumulative, and holistic.

Crime novelist and screenwriter Andrew Klavan was raised in a secular Jewish home that included some traditional ceremonial aspects of Judaism. Yet his home was entirely devoid of religious devotion. His father was essentially agnostic. "My mother," he writes, "was, to the day she died, as certain an atheist as I have ever met."[40] By the age of thirteen, Klavan had developed both a repulsion toward religion and a lifelong love of story. He sought to develop his own philosophy of life by experimenting with those he read about in what he calls the "tough guy" novels—books that exhibited existentialism, nihilism, and detachment—but he was unsettled by their incoherence and insufficiencies. "Just as I wanted my daydreams to make sense as stories," he says, "I wanted my personal philosophy to make sense too."[41]

The first turning point for Klavan was the realization that themes and symbols of certain high ideals pervaded the stories he loved most and that these ideals were rooted in Western Christianity. He recalls that by his midteens, he had already begun "to understand that at the heart of all Western mythology, all Western civilization, all Western writing, all Western thought, and every Western ideal, there stood a single book, the Bible, and a single man, Jesus of Nazareth."[42] He read the Bible, which, aside from the supernatural parts, he thought made sense as a metaphor. "As I struggled to educate myself and find my voice as a writer, the Bible story came to seem to me the story behind every story, especially the stories of the West. . . . It was, as the poet William Blake said, 'The Great Code of Art.'"[43] Eventually, Klavan fell in love with the Great Conversation of the Western canon, and he recoiled from postmodern attempts to deconstruct many of its principles, such as objective truth. Still, the philosophical incoherencies of relativism troubled him: "If after all, there is no truth, how could it be true that there is no truth? If there is no absolute morality, how can you condemn the

39. Garte also recounts one episode from his teen years, when he watched a film about the Gospel of Matthew with his girlfriend. He experienced what he now recognizes as a formative glimpse of the transcendent brought about by the piercing beauty of the film's musical score.

40. Andrew Klavan, "How a Man of the Coasts and Cities Found Christ," *Christianity Today*, August 22, 2016.

41. Andrew Klavan, *The Great Good Thing: A Secular Jew Comes to Christ* (Nelson, 2016), 88.

42. Klavan, *Great Good Thing*, 94.

43. Klavan, *Great Good Thing*, 106.

morality of considering my culture better than another?"[44] As a young man of only twenty, he was torn between the fashionable ideas of the day and what he believed, in his core, about the nature of reality. The brilliance and beauty of Western culture, he writes, "the poetry of Shakespeare and Keats, the music of Bach and Mozart, the painting and sculpture of Michelangelo and Raphael, and the novels of Cervantes, Zola, Tolstoy, and Dickens was somehow better, richer, and deeper than any other culture."[45] Reading Dostoevsky's *Crime and Punishment* was, as Klavan describes it, life-changing.

> After reading that novel, I was never quite the same. I did not accept the Christian aspect of it then. I couldn't. It was too alien to my upbringing, too at odds with the mental atmosphere in which I lived. I told myself that Dostoevsky was merely using Christ as a symbol for the reality of moral truth. But never mind. I knew beyond a doubt that the essential vision of the novel was valid. The story's rightness struck me broadside so that the journey of my heart changed direction . . . though I did not know it, though it took me decades, though I was lost on a thousand detours along the way—I was traveling away from moral relativism and toward truth, toward faith, toward God.[46]

Near the end of a long and excruciating season of psychosis and suicidal depression during which he had an intensely spiritual experience at the birth of his first child, Klavan entered a period of existential exploration. He searched for enlightenment in various ways. He sat in contemplative silence and experimental prayer in empty churches, he immersed himself in the meditative practices of Zen Buddhism, he became attracted to Freudian philosophy (thanks to his therapist), and then attempted to shoehorn his human experiences into an atheist framework. The philosophical reasoning he found in the likes of Nietzsche, Kafka, and Freud could not, however, make sense of the human condition or of Klavan's personal experiences of the world.[47]

What Klavan calls "the only truly nonlogical leap of faith I ever made" was his decisive assent to objective morality. This moved him back to agnosticism. After another decade, he became mentally healthy and gained success as a writer, all while being further shaped by both the reading and writing of stories. That's when he spontaneously prayed a simple prayer of

---

44. Klavan, *Great Good Thing*, 137.
45. Klavan, *Great Good Thing*, 214.
46. Klavan, *Great Good Thing*, 139.
47. In the work of the Marquis de Sade, Klavan encountered an atheism approached and articulated with logical consistency: No God equals no morality of any kind.

gratitude before falling asleep one night: "Thank you, God."[48] From that moment on, he cultivated a diligent prayer life: "I went on praying. I prayed every day. Every day, the joy of my joy grew more present to me. And God became more present to me as well."[49] This period of devoted theism went on for five years, culminating in an encounter with the Holy Spirit during a solitary scenic drive. Upon asking God what he should do next, the response was clear and startling: "Now, you should be baptized."[50] This led Klavan to consider the historicity of the Gospel accounts and then to assent to the truth of the resurrection while reading the Gospel According to Mark. Several months later, he was baptized in New York City.

In both Garte's and Klavan's conversion stories, we see a grand variety of factors that led them, over long spans of time, to the truth of theism and then to the truth of Christianity. We must consider how such observations should inform our philosophy of apologetics and encourage enrichment of the tool chest at our disposal. Of course, every nonbeliever we encounter is at a unique place in their journey, and thoughtful triage is necessary. Blessed is the one who is prepared and willing to meet a soul where they are and to participate in the Spirit's work.

Resources for Further Reading About Classical Apologetics

Dickinson, Travis. *Logic and the Way of Jesus: Thinking Critically and Christianly.* B&H, 2022.

Lewis, C. S. *Mere Christianity.* Reprint edition. HarperOne, 2000.

Lewis, C. S. *Surprised by Joy: The Shape of My Early Life.* Reprint edition. HarperOne, 2017.

Meyer, Stephen. *Return of the God Hypothesis: Three Scientific Discoveries that Reveal the Mind Behind the Universe.* HarperOne, 2021.

Rasmussen, Joshua. *How Reason Can Lead to God: A Philosopher's Bridge to Faith.* InterVarsity, 2019.

48. Klavan, *Great Good Thing*, 234.
49. Klavan, *Great Good Thing*, 239.
50. Klavan, *Great Good Thing*, 243.

Responses to Classical Apologetics

Evidential Apologetics Response

Sean McDowell

Classical and evidential apologetics have much in common. Both operate under the fundamental assumption that the Holy Spirit has granted image-bearers the capacity to reason about the truth of the God and Christianity. Both recognize the indispensable role of the Holy Spirit in guiding a non-believer to salvation. Both recognize the importance and value in offering positive evidences for the Christian faith—although, as we will see below, they differ methodologically about *how* to do so.

Before offering some reflections on the chapter, let me summarize (as best I can) the case offered for classical apologetics. Classical apologetics appeals to arguments from creation and reason to demonstrate God's existence and then defends the truths of special revelation based on historical evidences. In other words, classical apologists utilize natural theology *first* to argue for the existence of a Creator, and *then* offer historical evidences to argue specifically for Christianity.

Melissa Cain Travis offers two lines of defense. First, she points to examples of Christian thinkers throughout church history, up to the present, who assumed that natural revelation was one way we can attain knowledge about God. Second, she cites contemporary conversion accounts of people coming to the Christian faith *after* a long period of theism.

I have three responses to this chapter and then one final reflection about classical apologetics.

1. No scriptural case was made for classical apologetics.

Travis does mention Romans 1:20, but she offers no exegesis to show why this passage affirms the need for natural theology in evangelism and apologetics. Her historical survey shows that the traditional Christian view is that natural revelation is "one way that knowledge of God's existence may be attained." I agree! Yet recognizing natural revelation is different from emphasizing the need to appeal to arguments for the existence of God prior to offering evidence for Christ.

In Romans 1:18–21, Paul argues that all people have direct knowledge of God through creation; this knowledge is "clearly perceived." Thus arguments of natural theology are not *necessary* for people to "perceive" the evidence of a Creator. According to Paul, people don't reject such direct, universal knowledge of God because the evidence is unclear, but because of unrighteousness. Paul makes a similar argument from our awareness of the moral law in Romans 2:14–15. While our direct knowledge of God in creation can be developed into powerful, sophisticated arguments, natural theology is not required for awareness of the existence of a Creator and of our moral accountability to him.

The example of Augustine of Hippo supports my point. Travis cites a sermon in which Augustine points to the "great book" of nature revealing that "God made me." According to Augustine, God's existence is *obvious* in nature and *all people* have access to this knowledge. If so, then this raises some challenging questions for the classical apologist: If the existence of God is obvious and available to all people through nature, then why do we need natural theology? Why not directly offer evidence that *the God we know exists* has revealed himself in Christ?

My point is not to downplay the power of natural theology. I have co-written a book on Intelligent Design![1] I regularly utilize the arguments from fine-tuning, morality, and consciousness in my books, talks, and conversations with skeptics. Travis is right that natural theology has been a part of the history of the church, and she is right that it is (*fortunately*) experiencing a modern-day resurgence. Yet neither Scripture nor church history teaches that our evangelistic methodology must (or even should) involve a two-step process of classical apologetics. A two-step apologetic can be powerful, but it is not taught or modeled in Scripture as a principal method.

2. The Case for Christ *does not utilize arguments from natural theology.*

Travis cites the example of the conversion of Lee Strobel as part of her larger case. Ironically, Strobel's mega-selling book *The Case for Christ* does not

1. William A. Dembski and Sean McDowell, *Understanding Intelligent Design: Everything You Need to Know in Plain Language* (Harvest House, 2008).

utilize arguments from natural theology. Instead, it takes an evidential approach by offering historical arguments for the reliability of the Bible and the deity of Jesus without first establishing God's existence. Strobel may have come to faith through a diversity of evidence, arguments, and experiences—as Travis notes—but his wildly popular evangelistic book takes an evidential approach.

3. *Converts may not typically move through theism to Christianity.*

Travis notes that conversions often proceed through an initial phase of theism and, like C. S. Lewis's, involve a variety of experiential and intellectual stepping-stones. Agreed! Converts *often* move through theism to Christianity. But my suspicion is that *more often than not, they don't.* It seems that most people come to faith through hearing the gospel preached, encountering God in the Scriptures, hearing about the unique character and evidence for Jesus, or having a personal experience of God. For every example of someone coming to the Christian faith through theism, there are dozens of people coming directly to the Christian faith as a result of encountering Jesus, and this is also what we see in Scripture.

One final point: Although Travis did not argue this way, classical apologists often insist on making a case for theism before arguing for miracles. Why? Because, according to some classical apologists, one cannot invoke a miracle unless one has independent justification that a God exists who is capable of performing miracles. Such classical apologists recognize the persuasive value of evidential arguments. And yet, for the sake of consistency, they argue that one should first demonstrate the existence of God. While it is true that miracles are impossible if God does not exist, it does not follow that miracles must be regarded as impossible apart from a *demonstration* of God's existence. As long as the nonexistence of God has not been proven, miracles cannot be ruled out *a priori*. While arguments for the existence of God and the afterlife may increase the probability of a miracle, they are not biblically, methodologically, or philosophically necessary. The evidence for fulfilled prophecy, the conversion of Saul, modern miracles, and the resurrection of Jesus—the arguments that evidential apologists primarily invoke—can affirm both theism in general and Christianity in particular.

A PRIORI
(Latin, from what is before)
Knowledge acquired independent of any prior experience or observation.

Presuppositional Apologetics Response

James N. Anderson

Melissa Cain Travis defends the classical approach to apologetics that first deploys traditional natural theology to demonstrate God's existence and then offers historical evidential arguments to defend the truths of special revelation. I gladly concur with several points she makes in her chapter. I agree that our apologetic approach ought to be both *flexible* (adaptable to the specific beliefs and personal contexts of the individuals we engage with) and *holistic* (engaging different aspects of the human person). Travis rightly affirms that we can find "islands of common ground" for fruitful conversations based on common grace and humanity's creation in the image of God. I was also encouraged by her clear affirmation of the essential role of the Holy Spirit in apologetics. The conversion stories of Sy Garte and Andrew Klavan bear witness not only to the grace of God but also to the important role apologetics can play in people coming to faith in Christ.

Nevertheless, I do have some reservations about the classical approach as Travis characterizes and defends it.

1. Scripture should be our primary source.

My principal concern lies with the basis on which Travis defends her approach. She notes that a classical methodology can be defended "from a historical, philosophical, or theological perspective (or some combination thereof)." Surprisingly, for an evangelical Protestant, she opts for an almost entirely historical defense that appeals to the traditional position of the church on natural revelation supplemented with biographical accounts of contemporary Christian converts. No doubt, there is a proper place for historical arguments in Christian theology, but church tradition and the work of influential theologians and philosophers do not carry the authority and normative force of God's word.

It seems to me that any discussion of how Christians ought to defend the faith should *first* consider what Scripture has to say about the matter, either explicitly (as in, e.g., 1 Pet 3:15) or implicitly (considering what the Bible says about knowledge, reasoning, evidence, sources of truth, criteria for evaluating truth-claims, and so on). As a Presbyterian, I *could* argue that infant baptism has been the traditional majority position throughout the history of the church, but that wouldn't cut much ice with my Baptist friends. They want to be persuaded that infant baptism is supported *by*

Scripture—and rightly so! Travis cited only three biblical texts in her chapter (Rom 1:20; John 1:1–3; Gen 1:14) and little was said about any of them. This contrasts rather starkly with her extensive use of quotations from figures in church history. While much wisdom can be gleaned from the writings of the church fathers and other figures in church history, infallible Scripture should be our primary source.

2. Natural knowledge of God that Paul describes is immediate not inferential.

Of the three cited biblical texts, Romans 1:20 is the one most put to work. Travis correctly observes that the first chapter of Romans sets forth a robust doctrine of natural revelation and natural knowledge of God.[2] However, she makes the unjustified leap that Romans 1:20 therefore supports *natural theology*; i.e., "necessary preambles of the faith . . . that can be demonstrated by the light of natural reason, without any appeal to the special revelation of Scripture." Travis repeatedly conflates natural revelation and natural theology as though any biblical support for the former must also provide support for the latter. In reality, Romans 1 says little if anything about natural theology as classical apologists conceive it. The natural knowledge of God that Paul describes is more plausibly viewed as *immediate* rather than *inferential.* It is highly unlikely that a universally possessed knowledge of God would come through formal theistic arguments such as Thomas Aquinas's five ways. Moreover, Romans 1 speaks not only of the ubiquity and objective clarity of natural revelation, but it also speaks forcefully about the noetic effects of sin (Rom 1:18, 21–22, 28).[3] Travis has virtually nothing to say about the extent to which the human intellect has been corrupted by sin. This strikes me as a significant oversight.

3. Religious neutrality is philosophically and theologically untenable.

Travis rightly affirms that there is common ground between believers and unbelievers, but I would like to hear more about the nature of this common ground. Classical apologists frequently hold that this common ground must be religiously neutral to be acceptable to the unbeliever. Presuppositional apologists argue that religious neutrality is philosophically and theologically

2. Romans 1 implies not merely that "knowledge of God's existence is available to all" but that all *possess* knowledge of God. Cf. Moo's commentary on Romans referenced in Travis's chapter: They "possessed the truth of God but turned from it" (109).

3. See also the other biblical texts cited in the chapter on presuppositional apologetics.

untenable. I suggest there needs to be further engagement between the two camps on this point.

4. The monotheism of the Greek philosophers is not the monotheism of the Bible.

Travis apparently approves Justin Martyr's claim that the pagan Greek philosophers—and Socrates in particular—had reasoned to "the truth of monotheism." Yet the "monotheism" of Socrates, Plato, and Aristotle is a far cry from the monotheism of the Bible. If anything, such historical examples underscore the *limitations* of natural theology.

5. Presuppositional apologetics is more flexible and holistic.

If we're looking for a flexible and holistic approach, I would venture that presuppositionalism fits the bill better than the two-step approach of classical apologetics. Presuppositional apologetics can start with *any* aspect of ordinary human experience (truth, reason, sense perception, meaning, morality, beauty, science, and so on) and argue that a biblical theistic worldview is needed to account for it. Presuppositionalism also recognizes how the operation of the intellect is influenced by the will and the affections. As for the conversion stories of Garte and Klavan, it's not obvious they fit the classical approach of theism based on natural theology followed by historical evidences. Indeed, key elements of these testimonies will resonate with presuppositional apologists ("philosophical incoherence of materialist humanism," "philosophical incoherencies of relativism," "could not . . . make sense of the human condition or Klavan's personal experiences of the world").

In conclusion, my main concern with Travis's approach is *methodological*. I see no evidence that her classical approach is well grounded in biblical theology or Christian epistemology. Instead of THEOLOGY → EPISTEMOLOGY → APOLOGETICS, we are presented with HISTORY AND BIOGRAPHY → APOLOGETICS. Readers can judge for themselves which provides a firmer foundation.

Cultural Apologetics Response

D.A. Horton

The approach Melissa Cain Travis has articulated is well researched, nuanced, and well aligned with cultural apologetics, and it is readily available for readers to apply in any contemporary cultural setting. As someone raised with Pentecostal roots, it was refreshing to witness the intersection of intellectual depth with a complementary dependence on and reverence for the work of God the Holy Spirit. My response to Travis's content is filtered through the lens of how it can enhance my own application of cultural apologetics amid the nuanced demographics of my mission field—urban North America—and the university classroom.

I appreciate how Travis added the adjective *holistic* to her framing of classical apologetics as it lends affirmation to the whole humanity of the nonbeliever, not merely their spiritual or theological status—something I have personally neglected at times in evangelistic conversations. The appeal to pursue common ground and natural revelation allows all Christians in all places the opportunity to engage in ongoing apologetic evangelistic conversations. With North American culture rapidly distancing itself not only from a Judeo-Christian worldview but also from any explicit connection to Christianity, the chronology of the classical method reaches back into the archives of the Christian faith to a time when Christianity held no power or cultural authority—which is quite likely the same reality approaching those of us in North American contexts.

One comment I humbly make regarding this chapter has to do with making certain to mention the *African* identities of church fathers such as Athanasius of Alexandria and Augustine of Hippo. I have observed the sweeping North American movements toward decolonization and deconstruction thriving by dissecting the so-called Whiteness of dominant Eurocentric theological voices.[4] Movements such as the Hebrew Israelites, the Moorish Science Temple, the Nation of Gods and Earths, and the Nation of Islam have successfully attracted wavering hearts away from a reductive Eurocentric Christian faith, drawing them into a perspective that seems more ethnically inclusive. Additionally, they have leveraged historical evidence related to Christian support for racialization in their attempts to refute the claims of Christianity.

In Travis's summary of the North African bishop Athanasius's treatment of cosmic harmony, I found a bridge that connects her classical approach to a holistic cultural apologetics response to issues related to ethnicity and race. According to Travis, "the intricacy and diversity of created things existing

4. For a rebuttal of the notion that Christian orthodoxy is Eurocentric or inextricably tethered to Whiteness, see, e.g., Thomas Oden, *How Africa Shaped the Christian Mind: Rediscovering the African Seedbed of Western Christianity* (IVP, 2007).

in marvelous harmony are indicative of a single Creator God rather than many gods"—which beckons the listener to consider the harmony and order of God's design for the complexion of his global bride as described by Paul (Eph 2:11–18; 3:8–11).

I was inspired by the conversion narratives of Sy Garte and Andrew Klavan. As a professor at a university with a diverse student body, including many who do not follow Christ, I actively seek to include diverse voices from various professional backgrounds within the global church. I plan to incorporate the testimonies of Sy Garte and Andrew Klavan, in addition to the referenced works of Philip Melanchthon, into my teaching curriculum.

Ecclesial Apologetics Response

Timothy Paul Jones

I was delighted to read that Melissa Cain Travis recognizes—with Thomas Aquinas in *Summa contra gentiles*—that a two-step classical approach is not the only proper way to do apologetics.[5] Indeed, as Travis notes, there is no one-size-fits-all protocol for effective engagement with a nonbeliever. An effective apologetics strategy should engage not only the intellect but also the imagination, the conscience, aesthetic sensibilities, and humanity's intractable yearnings for meaningful narratives in formative communities. At the same time, any Christian apologetics strategy should be grounded first in exegesis of Scripture, and that brings me to two concerns with classical apologetics.

1. Paul was not describing rational inference of God's existence.

I am not convinced that Romans 1:20 can bear the weight that classical apologists place on Paul's words. Of course, classical apologists are in venerable company when they depict Romans 1:20 as an articulation of the possibility that we can rationally infer God's existence from the cosmos. Thomas Aquinas suggested as much in his exposition of Paul's letter to the Romans:

5. Thomas Aquinas reserved the two-step approach for engagement with persons who denied the authority of Scripture—Muslims and pagans in particular. See *Summa contra gentiles: Books I—II* (Emmaus, 2019), 1.2. The first three books of *Summa contra gentiles* defend the existence of one eternal, spiritual, perfect, omniscient, and sovereign deity based on natural reason; the fourth and final book argues for the truths of the Trinity, incarnation, sacraments, and resurrection based on Scripture and church tradition.

> God manifests something to humanity in two ways: one way is by endowing him with an inner light [*infundendo lumen interius*] through which he knows. . . . The other way is by propounding external signs of his wisdom, namely, sensible creatures. . . . Thus God manifested it to them either from within by endowing them with a light or from without by presenting visible creatures, in which, as in a book, the knowledge of God may be read. . . . The invisible things of God are known by the method of negation; the eternal power by the method of causality; the divinity by way of excellence.[6]

For Thomas, the knowledge of God described in Romans 1:20 is both immediate ("inner light") and inferred ("method of negation," "method of causality," "way of excellence"). Classical apologists have tended to follow this interpretive path, with a stronger emphasis on knowledge rationally inferred from creation.

Despite the respectable pedigree of this interpretation, John Calvin seems to me to have landed closer to the logic and grammar of the Spirit's inspired intention in this text. Here's how Calvin summarized Paul's teachings about humanity's response to natural revelation:

> We form a conception of divinity, and we conclude we are under the necessity of worshipping this being, whatever his character. Yet our judgment fails here before it discovers the nature or character of God. . . . We see only enough to keep us from making an excuse.[7]

Yes, natural revelation is one way that knowledge of God's existence may be attained. And yet, the knowledge of God that unregenerate humanity gains through the created order is not a rational observation that leads us to deduce the existence of the true God. This knowledge is, instead, an immediate awareness of a holy and ever-present deity; this awareness repels rebellious humanity, driving sinners to seek solace in the specious shelter of idolatry.

---

6. Thomas Aquinas, *Super epistolam ad Romanos,* in *Super epistolas Sancti Pauli*, ed. Raphaelis Cai, 8th ed. (Marietti, 1953), 1.6. It should be noted that not even Thomas attempted to defend the preambles of faith from the perspective of supposedly neutral common ground in a manner characteristic of modern thinking. Thomas made his presentation from the standpoint of a believer "who compares truths about God that he holds only thanks to the grace of faith and those truths about God that philosophers come to know by way of demonstrative proof." Ralph McInerny, Praeambula Fidei: *Thomism and the God of the Philosophers* (Catholic University of America Press, 2006), 30–31. See also Taylor, *Secular Age*, 294–95.

7. John Calvin on Romans 1:20–21, in *Ioannis Calvin Commentarii in Epistolam Pauli ad Romanos* (Vuedelinum Rihelium, 1540), microfilm. For further discussion of Calvin's perspective on humanity's natural knowledge of God, see Timothy Paul Jones, "John Calvin and the Problem of Philosophical Apologetics," *Perspectives on Religious Studies* 23 (1996): 392–95.

Until an individual surrenders to the supremacy of Jesus, this rebellious retreat will lead always and only to distorted thoughts and a darkened heart (Rom 1:21). The one destination to which our sense of deity will never lead, apart from the enlivening intervention of God's Spirit, is to a proper embrace of theism. That's not because God's revelation is deficient; it's because our minds are darkened and our reasoning is depraved. Instead of embracing the doctrine of God as it can be known through the created order, humanity universally trades gratitude and glory for a dreadful dungeon teeming with idols (Rom 1:21, 23). And yet, no matter how "deeply a human being may be sunk in degradation, he is conscious of the existence of God and of his duty to worship him."[8] Since our consciousness of God is immediate and innate, a child who knows nothing about deductive or inductive argumentation is no less aware of God's existence than the professional theologian. In the words of Calvin, "This is not a doctrine which is learned first in school. It is one of which each of us is a master from our mother's womb and one which nature itself allows no one to forget."[9]

In his novel *Blood Meridian*, Cormac McCarthy artfully portrays humanity's universal awareness of God's presence as a voice in the background that incessantly speaks "in the least of creatures," despite our protests and denials. "No man is give [*sic*] leave of that voice," an ex-priest in McCarthy's novel declares; and if this constant murmuring of God's self-revelation were ever to stop, you would "know you've heard it all your life."[10] And indeed, we would. "However far man wanders from God," Herman Bavinck noted, "he remains bound to heaven."[11]

2. *Bare theism is not progress.*

Even if our sense of divinity *did* lead to some form of monotheism, bare theism based on the witness of nature is not a forward progression in the direction of Christianity. Until and unless theists submit themselves to Jesus Christ as Lord, theism is nothing more than a lateral movement from one genus of idolatry to another. Deism and generic theism are not halfway houses between idolatry and Christianity; they are merely multiplications

8. Herman Bavinck, *Philosophy of Revelation*, ed. Cory Brock and N. Gray Sutanto (Hendrickson, 2018), 220.

9. John Calvin, *Institutio Christianae religionis*, in *Ioannis Calvini Opera Selecta*, vol. 3, ed. Peter Barth and Wilhelm Niesel (Kaiser, 1957), 1.4.3.

10. Cormac McCarthy, *Blood Meridian* (Vintage, 1992), 130–31.

11. Bavinck, *Philosophy of Revelation*, 220.

of more false gods with different names. "It is not of much concern whether you conceive of one God or of several," Calvin contended, "for you are continually departing from the true God and forsaking him. And, having left him, you have nothing that remains other than a damnable idol."[12]

Sometimes, God does save people through (or, perhaps more precisely, *from*) deism or mere theism, and I rejoice at the testimonies of C. S. Lewis, Sy Garte, and Andrew Klavan. At the same time, as long as their beliefs were bound in the spiritual quagmire of deism or theism, these individuals' commitments were nothing more than multiplications of idolatrous rebellions from which God in his grace set them free.

C. S. Lewis did—as Travis rightly points out—see theism as a possible stepping-stone in the direction of Christianity. Despite my deep affection for Lewis, I disagree with him that bare theism represents progress toward Christian faith. Still, it is worth noting that, even for Lewis, philosophical proofs never, by themselves, lead to religion. The function of classical arguments is to eliminate inhibitions that might prevent an individual's embrace of authentic faith, according to Lewis.[13]

I do not deny the cogency of classical arguments grounded in the natural order; the proofs themselves are sound. In my view, however, the greatest positive value of evidence from nature is not to turn skeptics into theists but to equip the church to recognize how every molecule in the cosmos points to the glorious beauty and rationality of our Triune God. In the words of Alister McGrath,

> Natural theology is not an individual undertaking; it is rooted in the life and ministry of the Christian community. Through faith, Christians develop habits of engagement with the natural world that allow it to be seen, understood, and evaluated in new ways. Such habits of thought are both generated and sustained by the Christian gospel, especially as this is proclaimed and embodied in the life of the church. . . . Natural theology can thus be

EMPIRICAL

(from Greek *empeirikos*, experienced)

Originating in or based on observation or experience.

12. Calvin, *Institutio*, 1.4.3. Stated in the positive, "A genuine Theism can never long remain a bare Theism." James Orr, *The Christian View of God and the World* (Regents Park, 2001), 76.

13. Lewis, "Is Theism Important?," 174–75. In another essay, Lewis recognizes that classical proofs are difficult to explain to non-Christians and noted that "fortunately, . . . people are usually disposed to hear the divinity of our Lord discussed before going into the existence of God." C. S. Lewis, "Christian Apologetics," in *C. S. Lewis Essay Collection and Other Short Pieces*, ed. Lesley Walmsley (HarperCollins, 2002), 157.

understood as the way in which the church "sees" the domain of nature. While beholding the same empirical realities as everyone else, the Christian community brings to this task its own distinct discipline of attention and framework of understanding. . . . It does not seek to prove God from nature, but affirms and welcomes the resonance . . . between its vision of reality and what is actually observed.[14]

14. Alister McGrath, *Darwinism and the Divine: Evolutionary Thought and Natural Theology* (Wiley, 2011), 285–86.

2

Evidential Apologetics

Sean McDowell

What is the best way to make the case for Christianity today? A wise strategy is to begin with the uniqueness of Christianity.

While there are several distinctions that separate Christianity from other religions, one of the key factors is that Christianity emphasizes the role of reason and evidence.[1] Jesus performed public miracles as signs that confirmed his identity. In contrast, Buddha reportedly said, "By this you shall know that a man is *not* my disciple—that he tries to work a miracle."[2] Eastern religions are about inner, personal experience rather than public evidence. Mormonism is about golden plates and Jesus visiting the Americas, which are verifiable in principle. Yet, when pressed with challenges to their faith, Mormons characteristically point to an inner personal experience, the "burning of the bosom," as the test for faith.[3]

In contrast to other faiths, Christianity is rooted in a public, testable historical event: the resurrection of Jesus. If Jesus did *not* rise from the dead, then Christianity is untrue and Christians are false witnesses about God (1 Cor 15:12–19). If Jesus *did* rise from the dead, then he is Lord and the Christian faith is true (Rom 1:3–4). The New Testament writers invite us to examine the evidence, follow the evidence, and then to proclaim it.

---

1. Craig Hazen lists four factors that distinguish Christianity from other faiths: (1) It is testable, (2) salvation is a free gift from God, (3) there is an amazing worldview fit, and (4) it has Jesus at the center. See Craig Hazen, "Christianity in A World of Religions," in *Passionate Conviction: Contemporary Discourses on Christian Apologetics*, ed. Paul Copan and William Lane Craig (B&H, 2007), 140–53.

2. Huston Smith, *The World's Religions* (HarperCollins, 1991), 97.

3. Book of Mormon, *Moroni* 10:4.

A Definition of Evidential Apologetics

Christianity is a religion founded in historical fact that is supported by the evidence. What does this mean for apologetics methodology? In practice, evidential apologists tend to favor a one-step approach from miracles and fulfilled prophecy to the truth of Christianity. Unlike classical apologists, who reason first for the existence of God and then to the truth of Christianity, evidential apologists believe miracles can serve as direct evidence for the supernatural.

Gary Habermas models this approach in his book *The Risen Jesus and Future Hope*. Habermas first rebuts David Hume's challenge to miracles and then offers his minimal facts approach to the resurrection. Afterward, in a chapter titled "A Theistic Universe," Habermas offers scientific and philosophical arguments against naturalism. He concludes that "the stronger the arguments become for a theistic universe, the clearer becomes the path that leads to Jesus's resurrection."[4] Habermas recognizes that theistic arguments help his overall case, but he puts them *after* the historical evidence. In *The Case for the Resurrection*, Gary Habermas and Michael Licona include some evidence for theism toward the end of the book when responding to naturalistic hypotheses, but long after presenting their historical case that Jesus has risen from the grave.

EVIDENTIAL APOLOGETICS

One-step apologetics method that moves from evidence for miracles and fulfilled prophecy to the truth of Christianity.

Although she argues for the reliability of the Gospels as a whole, rather than the minimal facts approach, Lydia McGrew also follows a similar methodology in *Testimonies to the Truth*. Her first chapters offer external confirmation to support factual statements within the Gospels. She concludes the book with a challenge to respond properly to the "real" Jesus of the Gospels who is both human and divine. While evidential apologists use a range of different kinds of positive evidence for the Christian faith, including arguments for the existence of God, they tend to lean heavily on making the historical case for Jesus and the Bible.

Evidential Apologetics vs. Evidentialist Epistemology

Evidential apologetics ought to be distinguished from evidentialist epistemology.[5] W. K. Clifford captures the heart of evidentialist epistemology with

4. Gary R. Habermas, *The Risen Jesus and Future Hope* (Rowman & Littlefield, 2003), 79.

5. For a recent defense of classical evidentialism as an epistemology, see John M. DePoe, "Classical Evidentialism," in *Debating Christian Religious Epistemology: An Introduction to Five Views on the Knowledge of God* (Bloomsbury Academic, 2020), 15–33.

the claim that "it is wrong, everywhere, always, and for anyone, to believe anything upon insufficient evidence."[6] Kenneth Boa and Robert Bowman formulate a comparable dictum for evidential apologetics—namely, that "it is wrong, everywhere, always, and for anyone, *to tell someone else* to believe something other than on the basis of evidence."[7] This doesn't mean that evidential apologists believe that one must always include evidences when sharing the gospel. What evidential apologists believe is that we shouldn't give the false impression that Christian faith can be separated from its factual basis.

Is Evidence Necessary for a Rational Faith?

Theological Rationalism

Evidential apologists differ over an important question: If Christianity is a faith founded on fact, then is a Christian irrational who does not understand—or cannot express—the factual basis of their beliefs? As an evidential apologist, Jonathan McLatchie embraces theological rationalism, which he defines as "the view that, generally speaking, the only way to have rational confidence in the truth of Christianity is by looking at the public evidence."[8] Although he concedes that there may be exceptional cases in which God makes his existence directly known to a believer in a way that warrants belief, this is not the norm.[9] McLatchie says that his faith in

6. William Kingdon Clifford, "The Ethics of Belief," in *An Anthology of Atheism and Rationalism*, ed. Gordon Stein (Prometheus Books, 1980), 282. Alvin Plantinga has claimed that classical foundationalism appears to be "self-referentially incoherent" since "it lays down a standard for justified belief that it doesn't itself meet." See Alvin Plantinga, *Warranted Christian Belief* (Oxford, 2000), 93. Evidentialists have offered two responses: (1) Modify the dictum slightly to say something like, "It is always a mistake to repose more confidence in a contingent proposition than is justified by the evidence one possesses." Some epistemologists consider epistemology as an *a priori* discipline. That is to say, true epistemic claims are necessarily true. Therefore, since this statement is not a contingent proposition, it does not fall within its own scope and there is no self-reference problem. (2) Claim that the arguments for evidentialism, alongside objections to major alternatives, *are* the evidence for evidentialism. My thanks to Jonathan McLatchie, in personal email correspondence (May 24, 2023), for these two responses.

7. Kenneth Boa and Robert Bowman, *Faith Has Its Reasons: Integrative Approaches to Defending the Christian Faith* (NavPress, 2001), 178.

8. Jonathan McLatchie, "A Defense of Theological Rationalism," July 14, 2018, https://jonathanmclatchie.com/a-defense-of-theological-rationalism/.

9. Jonathan McLatchie, "Why I Am an Evidentialist," June 30, 2020, https://jonathanmclatchie.com/why-i-am-an-evidentialist-a-brief-appraisal-of-apologetic-systems/.

Christ "rests on the public evidence alone, and not on any personal subjective experience."[10] And what about those who lack either the intelligence to grasp the arguments for the existence of God or access to apologetics training? Does this consign many Christians throughout history to irrationality? McLatchie believes that Christians can have a tacit or implicit rational justification for their beliefs when they intuitively recognize, for instance, how the complexity of living organisms points to an intelligent creator—even if this inference could not be verbally expressed. Likewise, Christians might read Isaiah 53 and identify the suffering servant as a prophecy about Jesus—even if they could not defend this interpretation against a learned Jewish rabbi such as Tovia Singer. Christians should not stay at this level of understanding, according to McLatchie, but such evidence-based reasoning is sufficient to have a rational faith.[11]

Self-Authenticating Witness of the Holy Spirit

In contrast to theological rationalism, William Lane Craig argues that the essential way believers know the truth of the Christian faith is through the inner witness of the Holy Spirit. Craig is not referring to an argument from religious experience but to a direct awareness through the testimony of the Holy Spirit that Christian theism is true. While Craig is a classical apologist (and only broadly an evidential apologist), his approach has been adopted by many evidential apologists.[12] On this approach, what is the task of apologetics? According to Craig, we *know* that Christianity is true through the direct testimony of the Holy Spirit, and we *show* the truth of Christianity through arguments and evidence.[13] In this view, understanding the factual basis of Christianity is not necessary for a rational faith.

A Mediating Position Between Theological Rationalism and Self-Authenticating Witness

Personally, I hold a mediating position between the two. Craig makes a convincing biblical case that the Holy Spirit gives believers immediate as-

10. McLatchie, "A Defense of Theological Rationalism."

11. McLatchie, "A Defense of Theological Rationalism."

12. Habermas, "An Evidentialist's Response," in *Five Views on Apologetics*, ed. Steven B. Cowan (Zondervan, 2000), 62.

13. William Lane Craig, *Reasonable Faith: Christian Truth and Apologetics*, 3rd ed. (Crossway, 2008), 43–52.

surance of their salvation. For instance, Craig points to 1 John 3:24 as indicating that "we know" that we abide in God and that God lives in us: "Whoever keeps his commandments abides in God, and God in him. And by this we know that he abides in us, by the Spirit whom he has given us."[14] People who have responded positively to the gospel, and who experience a direct assurance of their salvation through the testimony of the Holy Spirit, are hardly irrational in their faith.[15] Yet, as we will see below, Scripture also invites an examination of the public evidence, which acts as a basis for knowledge about God. For instance, Moses performed miracles so that the people would *know* that Yahweh is the one true God (Exod 7:5). And Jesus healed the paralytic so that onlookers would *know* that Jesus had divine authority (Mark 2:10). McLatchie seems fully justified in following the biblical pattern that miracles are a form of evidence that give knowledge, and hence rational justification, for faith.

In sum, believers can *know* Christian theism is true via the immediate testimony of the Holy Spirit, as Craig argues.[16] And yet believers can also *know* that Christianity is true through assessing the public evidence. It is not either/or. It's both/and. Nonetheless, all evidential apologists agree that we are to *show* our faith to others through evidence and arguments.

Now, let's turn to the task of examining what the Bible models about how we should advance the Christian faith.

---

14. Craig, *Reasonable Faith*, 45.

15. One area I differ with Craig regards his view that the testimony of the Holy Spirit is so warranted that it is an intrinsic defeater of any potential defeater that could be raised against it. Craig cites the example Plantinga references about a person who knows he is innocent of a crime even though the circumstantial evidence condemns him. Such a person is rational, according to Craig and Plantinga, even if they cannot refute the evidence. Yet is there really no point that such a person should change their views? What if the act was caught on camera? What if it was confirmed by DNA tests? Although it may be challenging to cite exactly what standard of evidence is required in this case, it seems unwarranted to remain impervious to any amount of evidence. If we expect Mormons to be open to evidence disconfirming their inner testimony of the Holy Spirit, then it seems we should be open to at least the possibility that we are mistaken.

16. If believers can know immediately that Christianity is true through the testimony of the Holy Spirit, then what about Mormons who claim to have an immediate authentication of their Scriptures? Craig has a response: "But how is the fact that other persons claim to experience a self-authenticating witness of God's Spirit relevant to *my* knowing the truth of Christianity via the Spirit's witness? The existence of an authentic and unique witness of the Spirit does not exclude the existence of false claims to such a witness. . . . Why should I be robbed of my joy and assurance of salvation simply because someone else falsely pretends, sincerely or insincerely, to the Spirit's witness?" Craig, *Reasonable Faith*, 49.

A Biblical Defense of Evidential Apologetics

Evidential Apologetics in the Old Testament

Elijah and the Prophets of Baal

During the time of King Ahab, Israel fell into great apostasy. King Ahab continued to commit the sins of Jeroboam and "did more to provoke the Lord, the God of Israel, to anger than all the kings of Israel who were before him" (1 Kgs 16:33). How would God restore the land? He called all of Israel to Mount Carmel to witness a public showdown between Elijah and the prophets of Baal. Elijah stood before the people and said, "How long will you go limping between two different opinions? If the Lord is God, follow him; but if Baal, then follow him" (1 Kgs 18:21). He then set up a public challenge in which he and the prophets of Baal would cry out for their gods to call down fire on their respective offerings. Whichever god answered by fire would be proven to be the true God (1 Kgs 18:24). Elijah mocked the prophets of Baal for hours as they cut themselves and cried out in futility. Then Elijah called all the prophets and people to come near as he prayed to God: "O Lord, God of Abraham, Isaac, and Israel, let it be *known* this day that you are God in Israel, and that I am your servant, and that I have done all these things at your word. Answer me, O Lord, answer me, that this people may *know* that you, O Lord, are God, and that you have turned their hearts back" (1 Kgs 18:36b-37; italics added). The offering was immediately burnt up, and the people began proclaiming that the Lord is God.

There is an important pattern in this account. First, the issue at stake was the identity of the one true God. How did God settle it? He prepared a public, supernatural showdown. Second, the miraculous event (evidence) gave the people *knowledge* about the identity of the true God ("know" and "known" both appear in the passage). Third, the people rightly believed in God after witnessing the miracle. Here is the pattern that emerges: (1) God does a miracle, which (2) gives the people knowledge, and (3) they respond with belief. They have knowledge about God because of the evidence and then they believe in him.

Miracles in Exodus

This same pattern can be seen hundreds of years earlier in the book of Exodus. To free the Israelites from slavery, God called up the prophet Moses as God's spokesman. How would Moses know that God would be with him?

God gave him the sign of turning his staff into a snake and restoring his hand from leprosy (Exod 4:1–9). How would the Israelites *know* that the Lord is the true God? He would deliver them from Egypt (Exod 6:7). How would the Egyptians *know* that Yahweh is the one true God? The judgment from the ten plagues (Exod 7:5).

Let's consider the purpose of the ten plagues. Here's why Moses turned the water in the Nile into blood: "Thus says the LORD, 'By this you shall *know* that I am the LORD'" (Exod 7:17). The same with the frogs. After Pharaoh requested the frogs be removed from the land, Moses said, "Be it as you say, so that you may *know* there is no one like the Lord our God" (Exod 8:10). As apologist Greg Koukl notes, this phrase appears at least ten times in the passage, which indicates it is a key theme of the story. In each case, God offered a miraculous sign (evidence), which gave the people knowledge (know), so they would obey (trust).[17] Exodus 14:31 brings this pattern full circle: "Israel *saw* the great power that the LORD used against the Egyptians, so the people feared the LORD, and they *believed* in the LORD and in his servant Moses."

Joshua Crossing the Jordan River

A third example is found in the story of Joshua crossing the Jordan River. How would the people of Israel *know* to trust Joshua as they trusted Moses? God says to Joshua, "Today I will begin to exalt you in the sight of all Israel, that they may *know* that, as I was with Moses, so I will be with you" (Josh 3:7). And then Joshua addresses the Israelites with the same promise: "Here is how you shall *know* that the living God is among you and that he will without fail drive out from before you the Canaanites, the Hittites, the Hivites, the Perizzites, the Girgashites, the Amorites, and the Jebusites" (Josh 3:10). At least three times in this short passage, God promises to give both Joshua and the people of Israel *knowledge* about his presence with them. How would he do it? A miraculous sign that provided evidence. In the case of Joshua, he stopped the flowing of the Jordan River so the people could walk through on dry ground (Josh 3:14–17). They saw the miracle with their own eyes; thus they *knew* that God was with Joshua as he had been with Moses, and so they trusted him too.

---

17. I am indebted to Greg Koukl for drawing my attention to this pattern in Exodus. See Greg Koukl, "Faith Is Not Wishing," *Solid Ground*, May 1, 2023, https://www.str.org/w/faith-is-not-wishing.

David and Goliath

As much as we like to root for an underdog, that is not the point of the biblical account of David and Goliath. As with the examples above, the point is about the identity of the one true God. Right before killing Goliath, David shouts out:

> You come to me with a sword and with a spear and with a javelin, but I come to you in the name of the Lord of hosts, the God of the armies of Israel, whom you have defied. This day the Lord will deliver you into my hand, and I will strike you down and cut off your head. And I will give the dead bodies of the host of the Philistines this day to the birds of the air and to the wild beasts of the earth, that all the earth may *know* that there is a God in Israel, and that all this assembly may *know* that the Lord saves not with sword and spear. For the battle is the Lord's, and he will give you into our hand. (1 Sam 17:45–47; italics added)

Although the defeat of Goliath may be a different kind of miracle than those in the stories of Elijah, Moses, and Joshua, it is still a remarkable (and supernatural) public feat that is meant to give the people knowledge that the God of Israel is the only God who saves.

Each of these four Old Testament stories helps illustrate the evidential nature of the Christian faith: God provides a miraculous sign (evidence), which gives the people knowledge (know), and then they believe.

Prediction of the Future and Provision of Witnesses

Throughout the Old Testament, God not only puts forth evidence that he is the one true God, but he summons those who worship false idols to present their case too. Specifically, he invites other deities to accurately predict the future so that we may see and *know* that only the true God's servants are genuine:

> Assemble yourselves and come; draw near together, you survivors of the nations! They have no knowledge who carry about their wooden idols, and keep on praying to a god that cannot save. Declare and present your case; let them take counsel together! Who told this long ago? Who declared it of old? Was it not I, the Lord? And there is no other god besides me, a righteous God and a Savior; there is none besides me. (Isa 45:20–21)

In this passage, God calls the nations to reject their false deities and accept him as the one true God. Why should they do this? The evidence. False deities can't predict the future (Isa 41:22). Thus false deities have no reliable witnesses (Isa 44:9). Yet Yahweh *can* predict the future and he *has* witnesses: "Behold, the former things have come to pass, and new things I now declare; before they spring forth I tell you of them" (Isa 42:9). Yahweh alone can predict the future. As a result, God calls Israel to be his witness to the world (Isa 44:7–8).

An evidential approach to faith appears in other passages in the Old Testament. For instance, God invites people to test his revelation. How do we distinguish a real prophet from a charlatan? By whether their predictions always come true (Deut 18:21–22). The Old Testament emphasizes that Yahweh is the one true God, worthy of worship, who has made himself known to the world through miraculous deeds. He has raised up Israel, in part, to be his witness to the world.

Evidential Apologetics in the New Testament

The New Testament continues this evidential approach to faith. Four key points need to be emphasized.[18]

Believers are encouraged to test religious claims with evidence and reason

Consider three examples from Jesus, Paul, and John:

> Jesus: "Beware of false prophets, who come to you in sheep's clothing but inwardly are ravenous wolves. You will *recognize* them by their fruits" (Matt 7:15; italics added).[19] According to Jesus, we need to test the claims of various prophets by whether their teachings lead to repentance (Matt 21–24).
>
> Paul: "Do not quench the Spirit. Do not despise prophecies, but *test everything*; hold fast what is good" (1 Thess 5:19; italics added). Paul is encouraging the Thessalonians to test the legitimacy of prophecy. Don't accept prophecy blindly. Test it. Examine the facts.
>
> John: "Beloved, do not believe every spirit, but *test the spirits* to see whether they are from God" (1 John 4:1; italics added). We know prophecies are from God, according to John, if they proclaim an accurate view of Jesus (John 2–3).

---

18. I am indebted to J. Warner Wallace for modeling this evidential approach in his book *Forensic Faith: A Homicide Detective Makes the Case for a More Reasonable, Evidential Christian Faith* (David C. Cook, 2017), 41–53.

19. See Sean McDowell, "Should Experience Trump Scripture?," March 22, 2016, https://seanmcdowell.org/blog/should-experience-trump-scripture.

> If a spirit does not confess that Jesus has come in the flesh, reject it as the spirit of the antichrist.

The New Testament consistently urges believers to test and examine their beliefs with reason and evidence.

Jesus Performed Miracles to Confirm His Identity

There is a striking consensus among New Testament scholars that Jesus performed miracles to demonstrate the arrival of God's kingdom and that the messianic age had begun.[20] Although Jesus had compassion on people, his primary reason for performing miracles was to confirm the authenticity of his message.

In Mark 2, four men bring a paralytic to Jesus. Because the house is so crammed with people that they cannot get him inside, they lower the paralytic through the roof. When Jesus sees their faith, he pronounces that the man's sins have been forgiven. But of course, that's *not* why he came. After castigating the scribes for questioning his authority, Jesus then heals the man. But right before doing so, he indicates why he would perform the miracle: "'But that you may *know* that the Son of Man has authority on earth to forgive sins'—he said to the paralytic— 'I say to you, rise, pick up your bed, and go home'" (Mark 2:10; italics added).

As in the above examples from the Old Testament, a miracle acts to confirm divine identity. Jesus performed a miracle (evidence), which gave the people knowledge about God (know), and they responded in belief.

In his debates with the religious leaders in the Gospel of John, Jesus points to multiple witnesses as confirmation of his divine authority. He points to his miracles (John 5:36), the witness of the Father (5:37), the witness of the Scriptures (5:39), and the testimony of Moses (5:46). When the Jews press him for a sign, he points to his resurrection: "Destroy this temple, and in three days I will raise it up" (John 2:19b). The Jews are confused because they think he is referring to the Jerusalem temple. But the disciples later recall this prediction, after he has risen, and believe the Scriptures and the words of Jesus (John 2:20–22).

When John the Baptist experienced doubt in prison, Jesus encouraged him to remember the positive evidence that he was in fact the Messiah. When John's disciples inquired of Jesus, he responded: "Go and tell John

20. Craig L. Blomberg, *Can We Still Believe in God? Answering Ten Contemporary Challenges to Christianity* (Brazos Press, 2020), 50–51.

what you have seen and heard: the blind receive their sight, the lame walk, lepers are cleansed, and the deaf hear, the dead are raised up, the poor have good news preached to them" (Luke 7:22). In other words, the evidence should give John confidence that Jesus is the expected one.

With both believers and nonbelievers, Jesus performed miracles as confirmation of his identity and divine authority.

Jesus Commissioned His First Followers to Be Witnesses to What They Had Seen and Heard

Right before his ascension, Jesus told his disciples that they would soon receive the power of the Holy Spirit so they would be his "witnesses in Jerusalem and in all Judea and Samaria, and to the end of the earth" (Acts 1:8). The book of Acts records the apostles fulfilling this command:

> This Jesus God raised up, and of that *we are all witnesses*. (Acts 2:32; italics added).

> But you denied the Holy and Righteous One, and asked for a murderer to be granted to you, and you killed the Author of life, whom God raised from the dead. To this *we are witnesses*. (Acts 3:14–15; italics added)

> But Peter and John answered them, "Whether it is right in the sight of God to listen to you rather than to God, you must judge, for we cannot but *speak of what we have seen and heard*." (Acts 4:19–20; italics added)

> [Jesus] went about doing good and healing all who were oppressed by the devil, for God was with him. And *we are witnesses* of all that he did both in the country of the Jews and in Jerusalem. (Acts 10:38–39; italics added)

Outside the book of Acts, the apostles also witness to what they had seen and heard about Jesus. Paul appeals to his own authority as a witness to the risen Jesus (1 Cor 9:5). John testifies to what he has "seen and heard" (1 John 1:1–3). And Peter claims that he was "a witness of the sufferings of Christ" (1 Pet 5:1).

Jesus Expects Followers Today to Proclaim an Evidential Faith

Along with preaching and healing, Jesus reasoned with people and gave evidence to confirm his identity. The apostles also reasoned with people and spoke as witnesses to what they had seen and heard. Church fathers of the second century, such as Justin Martyr (c. 100–c. 165), Athenagoras

(c. 133–c. 190), and Tertullian (c. 155–c. 220) are called "apologists" because they defended and advanced the Christian faith. Specifically, in his *Dialogue with Trypho the Jew,* Justin utilizes the evidence of fulfilled prophecy to support Jesus being the Messiah.[21] We are to follow their example today by proclaiming the evidence that points to Jesus as Messiah and Lord and by being ready with an answer for our hope (1 Pet 3:15).

Common Objections to Evidential Apologetics

Before we conclude this section, it is important to engage four common questions about evidential apologetics.

1. Didn't Jesus Advocate Faith Without Evidence?

The interaction between Jesus and Thomas is often held up as a model of why blind faith is preferable to an evidence-based faith. When Thomas refuses to believe without seeing and touching Jesus's hands and side, Jesus responds by saying, "Blessed are those who have not seen and yet believe" (John 20:29b). Does this mean the demand for evidence is misguided?

This question assumes that seeing and touching are the only kinds of relevant evidence. Thomas had sufficient evidence to believe Jesus had risen, but he still refused to believe.[22] While future generations are not able to see and touch Jesus as Thomas was, they are still invited to an evidence-based faith. The next verses in the Gospel of John make this clear: "Now Jesus did many other signs in the presence of the disciples, which are not written in this book; but these are written so that you may believe that Jesus is the Christ, the Son of God, and that by believing you may have life in his name" (John 20:30–31).

2. Does Evidence Actually Convince Anyone?

The Bible is full of examples of people seeing miracles and then believing. For instance, many Jews believed when Jesus raised Lazarus from the dead

---

21. For examples, see chap. 51 in *Dialogue with Trypho*. Trypho argues that the prophecies of Christ are ambiguous, and Justin identifies clear and specific scriptural promises that Christ fulfilled.

22. First, Thomas had the eyewitness testimony of the other ten disciples. Eight days earlier, Jesus had appeared when Thomas was elsewhere. Second, Thomas had heard Jesus predict that he would die and rise again (see Mark 8:31; 9:31; 10:33–34). Yet Thomas still refused to believe.

(John 11:45).[23] While helping update his classic book *Evidence That Demands a Verdict*, I was able to ask my father, Josh McDowell, about the role evidence played in his personal journey to faith. He credits the evidence as leading him to consider the claims of Christ, but it was an understanding of the love of God, through the power of the Holy Spirit, that ultimately drew him to faith.[24] No one is argued into the kingdom, just as no one is loved into the kingdom. Rather, evidence is one tool the Holy Spirit often uses in bringing people to faith.

3. Isn't It More Effective to Combine Natural Theology and Evidence?

According to William Lane Craig, Christian evidence is "most effective when combined with the arguments of natural theology."[25] Is it most effective to combine them in debate? Yes, and no one would know better than Craig. Is it most effective for responding to skeptics? Yes, there is force in a cumulative case for Christianity that incorporates philosophical, scientific, and historical arguments. As noted above, evidential apologists often incorporate evidence for theism when responding to naturalistic hypotheses for the resurrection.

Is it more effective to combine natural theology with evidence in evangelism? Not necessarily.[26] *The Case for Christ* and *More Than a Carpenter*

---

23. See also John 11:48; Acts 9:35, 9:42, and 13:12. Credit to Brian Morley for this insight in his *Mapping Apologetics: Comparing Contemporary Approaches* (InterVarsity Press, 2015), 32.

24. Josh McDowell and Sean McDowell, *Evidence That Demands a Verdict* (Nelson, 2017), xxiii.

25. William Lane Craig, "A Classical Apologist's Response," in *Five Views on Apologetics*, 128.

26. Some classical apologists have argued that the move from a historical argument to God is illegitimate. For example, see Norman L. Geisler, *Christian Apologetics* (Baker, 1976), 95–96. In response, Jonathan McLatchie offers a helpful distinction between the impossibility of miracles apart from the existence of God and the impossibility of identifying a miracle apart from an independent demonstration of the existence of God. Miracles are impossible if God does not exist, but the existence of God need not necessarily be demonstrated before a miracle could be detected, and thus act as evidence for theism. Or put differently, a lack of independent demonstration of God's existence does not entail a zero-prior probability of God performing a miracle, which means that, in principle, a miracle cannot be ruled out before a consideration of the evidence. See Jonathan McLatchie, "Why I Am an Evidentialist." In personal correspondence (May 24, 2023), McLatchie shared this analogy to clarify his point: "Consider the hypothesis that a particular individual (let's call him John Smith) exists. To what extent does evidence for the truth of this hypothesis raise the prior probability that I will receive an email from John Smith tomorrow afternoon? It does bear positively on

have been two of the most effective evangelism tools over the past half century and neither of them utilizes natural theology. Instead, they both focus on advancing the testimonial evidence for Jesus apart from a prior demonstration of the existence of God.[27] Although C. S. Lewis begins *Mere Christianity* with an appeal to the existence of an objective moral law, and hence a moral law giver, he notes, "Fortunately, though very oddly, I have found that people are usually disposed to hear the divinity of Our Lord discussed *before* going into the existence of God."[28] The arguments of natural theology are powerful and effective for debate and in responding to skeptics, but they are not necessarily the most effective for evangelism.

4. Does That Mean We Need to Always Share the Evidence?

No, there is power in preaching the gospel alone (John 5:24; 1 Cor 2:1–5). There is power in the word of God (Heb 4:12). There is power in the testimony of a changed life (John 9:25). Like Jesus, we should tell stories that appeal to the imagination.[29] One of the reasons books like *The Case for Christ* and *More Than a Carpenter* are such effective tools for evangelism is that Strobel and McDowell use their personal, dramatic stories of conversion to frame the evidence.

One of my most popular blogposts is my list of top books to give a non-Christian.[30] The first "book" I recommend is the Gospel According to John. My goal is to get seekers into Scripture first, and *then*, if they are open to it, invite them to consider the evidence. We don't always need to give evidence when sharing the gospel, but we shouldn't give the false impression that the Christian faith can be separated from its factual basis.

---

the prior, but it is only negligible. However, supposing we had no independent evidence for John Smith's existence, the fact that I *do* in fact receive an email from John Smith tomorrow afternoon greatly increases the probability that John Smith does in fact exist. In a similar way, the existence of God does negligibly raise the probability of the resurrection, but evidence supporting that God raised Jesus from the dead greatly raises the probability of theism."

27. In the 2009 update of *More Than a Carpenter*, I added a small chapter on the evidence from natural theology. That chapter, "The New Atheism," functions primarily as a rebuttal of the arguments of the new atheists that science is against faith. See Josh McDowell and Sean McDowell, *More Than a Carpenter*, rev. ed. (Tyndale, 2009), 45–62.

28. C. S. Lewis, "Christian Apologetics," in *God in the Dock*, ed. Walter Hooper (Eerdmans, 1970), 100.

29. Holly Ordway, "The Value of Storytelling for Apologetics," in *A New Kind of Apologist*, ed. Sean McDowell (Harvest House, 2016), 111–17.

30. Sean McDowell, "What Are the Top Books to Give a Non-Christian?," February 29, 2016, https://seanmcdowell.org/blog/what-are-the-top-books-to-give-a-non-christian.

Resources for Further Reading About Evidential Apologetics

Gould, Paul, ed. *Four Views on Christianity and Philosophy.* Zondervan, 2016.

McDowell, Josh, and Sean McDowell. *Evidence that Demands a Verdict: Life-Changing Truth for a Skeptical World.* Nelson, 2017.

McDowell, Josh, and Sean McDowell. *More than a Carpenter.* Rev. ed. Tyndale, 2009.

McGrew, Tim. *The Foundations of Knowledge.* Rowman & Littlefield, 1995.

McGrew, Tim, and Lydia McGrew. *Internalism and Epistemology: The Architecture of Reason.* Routledge, 2016.

Responses to Evidential Apologetics

Classical Apologetics Response

Melissa Cain Travis

Evidential apologetics, as articulated by Sean McDowell above, is a methodology that wonderfully showcases the rationality and testability of Christianity. The one-step method typically preferred by its proponents can be highly effective, given the powerful evidence we have at our disposal for the reliability of the Gospel accounts, the historicity of Jesus of Nazareth, and the pivotal moment of our Savior's resurrection from the dead. It is not unreasonable to support this evidential case with classical arguments for mere theism *ex post facto*; those with whom we dialogue are, after all, likely to consider the arguments and evidence collectively.

McDowell's clarification about the difference between evidential apologetics and evidentialist epistemology is important, because it helps readers to avoid a common caricature of the evidential perspective—that its proponents believe the only legitimate form of evangelism is that which provides *evidence* for Christianity. Quite the contrary! The evidential apologist readily acknowledges that a simple presentation of the gospel message can be fruitful. In other words, they are not limiting the Holy Spirit to one mode of operation in the pursuit of a soul.

In his Old Testament case for evidential apologetics, McDowell cites several instances in which the knowledge and exclusivity of the Hebrew God was confirmed by direct experience of the miraculous as well as the fulfillment of prophecy. His New Testament case then points to the exhortations of Jesus, Paul, and John to test religious claims—such as prophecies—using observation and reason, the miraculous signs performed by Jesus, and the Great Commission to his disciples, who were eyewitnesses of the Messiah.

While this collective biblical data affirms, in a general sense, the importance and legitimacy of evidential knowledge, there seems to be a vulnerability with respect to one category of biblical data. One might argue that biblical examples of knowledge obtained by direct observation of supernatural activity are not sufficiently analogous to the use of historical records to serve as support for contemporary evidential apologetics. This objection is founded upon the difference between *deriving knowledge from a sensory experience* (such as the Israelites witnessing the Exodus miracles) and *reasoning inferentially from historical data* (such as written eyewitness accounts and other kinds of records) *to a propositional fact* (Jesus rose from the dead). The use of fulfilled prophecy as evidence for the truth of Christianity is less impacted by this vulnerability, since records of messianic prophecies and their fulfillment in the person and life of Jesus were already a matter of historical evidence during the post-ascension era documented in Acts and the New Testament Epistles.

In the penultimate section of his chapter, McDowell addresses common questions about evidential apologetics. His responses are concise and valuable, but there are a couple of statements that might benefit from clarification or further nuance. He asserts that we cannot argue someone into the kingdom of God, but that the Holy Spirit sometimes uses evidence in bringing someone to faith; this is an observable fact. He then rightfully concedes the power of a cumulative case that includes the arguments of natural theology, but he says this is "not necessarily" more effective than the one-step evidential apologetics strategy in an evangelistic context. By "not necessarily," does he simply mean we *don't know* which one is more effective? Or does he mean that a cumulative case *may be more effective* than one-step evidential apologetics in some evangelistic conversations but not in all or most? The diversity of contemporary conversion accounts certainly attests to the fact that there is no one-size-fits-all method.

Overall, the methodology of evidential apologetics, as described by McDowell, does not contradict holistic classical apologetics, which affirms the enormous value of reason and evidence and recognizes that arguing directly for Christianity at the outset may be highly effective in some cases. Where the two methods differ is in their *scope.* Classical apologetics includes, but is not limited to, the tools and strategies of the evidential apologist. Perhaps one might say, then, that the classical apologist has greater flexibility when it comes to encounters with individuals whose minds remain closed to the reality of the supernatural despite the historical evidence.

Presuppositional Apologetics Response

James N. Anderson

Sean McDowell defends the one-step approach of evidential apologetics, arguing directly from miracles and prophecy to the truth of Christianity. In contrast to the two-step approach of classical apologists, evidential apologists see no need to employ natural theology to demonstrate God's existence before making historical evidential arguments in defense of the factual basis of Christianity. The centerpiece of their apologetic for Christianity is a historical case for the resurrection of Jesus: As McDowell put it, "If Jesus *did* rise from the dead, then he is Lord, and the Christian faith is true."

Happily, I found much to agree with in McDowell's chapter. The Bible does indeed emphasize the role of reason and evidence in evaluating truth-claims, and miracles in particular are presented as providing evidential grounds for faith (John 20:30–31). I appreciate that evidential apologists like McDowell want to argue directly for Christian distinctives, such as the resurrection of Christ, rather than using generic theism as a stopover. McDowell wisely distances himself from theological rationalism, which would put knowledge of the truth of Christianity beyond the reach of most ordinary Christians. I was also delighted to read in his chapter that Christianity can be known to be true via the internal testimony of the Holy Spirit, that "there is power in preaching the gospel alone," and that the first book he recommends for a non-Christian is John's Gospel. Above all, I applaud the fact that McDowell makes his case for evidential apologetics *primarily from Scripture*, assembling a wide range of biblical texts that illustrate the evidential nature of the Christian faith. To all of this I say, "Amen!" Unsurprisingly, however, I must also register some points of disagreement between us.

1. The limitations of human reasoning and the corrupting effects of sin on the human intellect were not recognized.

While the Bible unquestionably endorses the use of reason and evidence, it also has sobering things to say about the limitations of human reasoning and the corrupting effects of sin on the human intellect. I didn't find any recognition of the latter in McDowell's chapter. This points to a more general problem with his approach: He correctly identifies *some* elements of a biblical epistemology (e.g., that evidence can often serve as the basis for knowledge and for testing truth-claims), while overlooking many *other* significant things that Scripture has to say about epistemological matters (e.g., about the relationship between general and special revelation, the noetic effects of sin, and the authority and self-attesting nature of Scripture).

2. The Spirit also testifies to the divine authorship of Scripture.

McDowell makes room for the internal testimony of the Holy Spirit, but he fails to mention that the Spirit also testifies *to the divine authorship of Scripture*. It's not as though the Spirit imparts a direct knowledge of the truth of Christianity independently of the biblical witness. The Protestant tradition has always affirmed that the Spirit and the word work together to bring about a saving knowledge of God.[1] I suspect McDowell would agree, but this point is conspicuously absent from his discussion.

3. The resurrection is not sufficient to vindicate the entire Christian faith.

I have concerns about the evidentialist impulse to hang everything on a historical case for the resurrection of Christ—the idea being that, if we can only show that Jesus rose from the dead, then we have thereby vindicated the entire Christian faith. The resurrection is necessary for the truth of Christianity (1 Cor 15:14, 17) but far from sufficient. There are pseudo-Christian cults that also affirm the historicity of the resurrection accounts. Indeed, I see no reason why a Hindu or Buddhist couldn't accommodate the *historical fact* of the resurrection. What's really at stake here is the *meaning* of the resurrection, and that depends crucially on other essential tenets of a Christian worldview that are known by special revelation.[2]

4. Evidences are always interpreted.

This leads to a related point: No one approaches historical or empirical evidences from a neutral, unbiased, presuppositionless stance. Evidences don't simply speak for themselves. Evidences are always *interpreted* in terms of a person's prior worldview. I suspect that when McDowell hears eyewitness reports of weeping statues, levitating shamans, or extraterrestrial visitations, he interprets them through the lens of his Christian worldview (and rightly so). Likewise, the heinous evils and seemingly pointless suffering we observe in the world. The point is not that appeals to evidence are inappropriate or ineffective, but rather that they need to be accompanied by arguments establishing the proper presuppositions by which to interpret the evidence.

---

1. See, e.g., *Westminster Confession of Faith*, 1.5.

2. Contra McDowell, Rom 1:3–4 does not say that the resurrection proved Jesus to be the Son of God. His disciples knew he was the Son of God well before the resurrection (Matt 16:16). Rather, Paul's point is that Jesus's resurrection signified a transition from his state of humiliation to his state of exaltation: "the Son of God *in power*" (italics added).

5. The biblical arguments presented do not establish anything distinctive about evidential apologetics.

McDowell makes a strong case from a range of Scriptures that the Christian faith is supported by evidence, that evidence often serves as the basis for knowledge about God, that Jesus performed miracles as confirming evidence of his claims, and that Christians should proclaim "an evidential faith." But which of the other contributors would disagree with any of that? Both classical apologists and presuppositional apologists will certainly want to affirm the important role that evidence plays. McDowell's biblical arguments don't seem to establish anything *distinctive* about the evidential approach he advocates.

6. Prior divine revelation is the primary criterion when testing purported later revelations.

While it is true that the Bible endorses appeals to evidence, it also bears witness to the limitations of empirical evidence in bringing about a change of beliefs (Matt 11:23–24; 12:24; Luke 16:27–31; John 11:47–48). Moreover, when testing purported divine revelations, the *primary* criterion is *prior* divine revelation (Isa 8:20; Acts 17:11; Gal 1:8–9; 1 Thess 5:20–21; 1 John 4:1–3).

Let me finish with a conciliatory word. If evidential apologetics is simply the idea that "we are to *show* our faith to others through evidence and arguments," then count me in! In fact, I would argue presuppositional apologetics is the *most* evidential, since presuppositional apologists hold that *everything*—from the miraculous to the mundane—is evidence for the truth of Christian theism when properly interpreted. We would simply insist on two things: First, that our apologetic should engage with *both* evidence *and* the presuppositions we bring to the evidence; and second, that the Bible *evidences itself* to be God's word.[3]

Cultural Apologetics Response

D.A. Horton

In the spirit of full disclosure, I must acknowledge feeling anxious early in the chapter when McDowell introduced his one-step evidential apologetics method as an approach grounded in miracles. In this era of skepticism, my

3. *Westminster Confession of Faith*, 1.5.

central concern was that prospective listeners to such an approach might potentially disregard his argument as entirely subjective and not verifiable through objective methods. I found comfort, however, in McDowell's intermediary stance, which seeks to harmonize the inner witness of the Holy Spirit with the logical analysis of public evidence. For educators engaging with skeptical students and for pastors guiding individuals who may be questioning God's existence, McDowell's approach provides reassurance that the Holy Spirit can guide us in grounding the evidence of the Christian worldview. This guidance draws from personal experience, philosophy, the natural and social sciences, natural theology, and so on.

The author's distinction between evidential apologetics and evidentialist epistemology was admirable as well. The texts from the Old and New Testaments provided a framework for understanding his argument, ultimately showcasing how Christ employed evidence when engaging with John the Baptist and Thomas. This viewpoint allowed me to interpret the teachings of the John the evangelist (John 20:30–31) in a fresh and stimulating manner.

Sean McDowell's chapter reminded me of the importance of faithfully focusing on the resurrection when engaging people from diverse ethnicities and subcultures. In some cases, these engagements can tend to reduce conversations about Christianity to discussions about the Black/White binary or about colonial systems of socioeconomic oppression. Inviting my interlocutors to explore the historical evidence of Jesus's resurrection and then to engage reliable testimonies from Asiatic and African patristic voices allows them to see not only that Jesus is alive but also that he is actively building a multicultural, multiethnic, multilingual, and multigenerational church—a process that began on Pentecost (Acts 2) and continues still today.

Ecclesial Apologetics Response

Timothy Paul Jones

Evidential apologetics was the first apologetics method I embraced as my own. My first couple of apologetics books were written as an evidential apologist. Today, the verificational aspect of my work still carries a deep evidential imprint.[4] As such, I was unsurprised to find that I wholeheartedly agree

4. For my early defense of evidential apologetics, see, e.g., Timothy Paul Jones, *Conspiracies and the Cross* (Frontline, 2008), 5–11. Research in patristics turned my thinking in an ecclesial direction, as exemplified by my chapter later in this book, while deeper engagement

with the majority of Sean McDowell's chapter. As a confessional Reformed apologist, I particularly appreciated his recognition that evidence can never cause anyone to believe. Saving faith is not a human act in response to evidence but a divine gift worked in the human heart by the Holy Spirit (see Eph 2:8). Evidence is one tool through which the Spirit may work to bring a sinner to faith, but evidence is never a sole cause or sufficient condition for faith.

Still, despite many points of concurrence, I did note one point of critique and one point in need of clarification as I read the chapter.

1. Not all of the biblical examples provide support for evidential apologetics.

First, my critique: Although Scripture does indeed include many examples of evidence being provided, these provisions of evidence do not necessarily constitute support for evidential apologetics. Every apologist, regardless of their preferred method, agrees that Scripture commands Christians to be prepared to provide evidence for their Christian hope (1 Pet 3:15). The practice of evidential apologetics is, however, more than merely a proclamation of a well-evidenced hope. Evidential apologetics is, as McDowell notes, a distinctive one-step approach that moves from miracles and fulfilled prophecies to the truth of Christianity. And yet, not all the biblical examples included in McDowell's chapter necessarily support the stated method. In their contexts, some of the biblical examples have more to do with assuring the covenant community of God's faithfulness than with providing evidence for the community's hope (Josh 3:1–17; 1 Sam 17:45–47). Other examples center primarily on the rationale for the apostles' persistent obedience (Acts 4:19–20). In all these examples, God does undeniably supply evidence. Yet a divine supply of evidence is not the same as biblical support for evidential apologetics. Evidential apologetics encompasses not only the evidence itself but also a particular set of assumptions regarding the nature, justification, and application of the evidence.

2. Moving from miracles to the truth of Christianity depends more on preexisting commitments than on the quality of the evidence.

Now for a point of clarification, the goal of which is to fill a possible gap in this presentation of evidential apologetics. Evidential apologetics moves in

with the works of Francis Schaeffer and Herman Bavinck inclined me toward an approach that is verificational and broadly presuppositional.

a single step from miracles and fulfilled prophecies to the truth of Christianity. And yet, there's an important aspect of this step that seems to be underemphasized in the chapter. This missing aspect has to do with the *interpretation* of the evidence. Any movement from miracles and fulfilled prophecy to the truth of Christianity requires interpretation of miraculous phenomena and textual testimonies, yet McDowell's defense of evidential apologetics seems to brush over this intervening hermeneutical act.

The intervening hermeneutical act that stands between the experience of miracles and our apprehension of the truths to which they point is highly significant. There are, after all, no uninterpreted facts in history; everything we perceive as historical fact is interpreted. How people understand the Christian evidence for miracles and fulfilled prophecies always depends on the preexisting commitments and communities by which these individuals are making sense of their lives. That was true in ancient times, and it's still true today. "It is impossible to reason based on brute facts. Everyone who reasons about facts comes to those facts with a schematism into which he fits the facts."[5]

HERMENEUTICS
(from Greek *hermēneutikos*, pertaining to interpretation) Branch of knowledge that deals with interpretation, especially of the Bible or literary texts.

One example of this truth is as near as your New Testament. Some first-century witnesses glimpsed the risen Lord Jesus with their own eyes, yet they did not immediately interpret what they saw as evidence for a miraculous resurrection (Matt 28:17). Why did they hesitate? They doubted, at least in part, because their internal narratives and intellectual schematizations had not yet been reconfigured to include the hope of a divine Messiah, crucified and raised from the dead.[6] Even if someone witnessed the results of a miracle firsthand, the intellectual transition from the perception of a supernatural event to the divine truth implied by the event required processes of interpretation shaped by preexisting expectations.

5. Cornelius Van Til, *Christian Theistic Evidences*, ed. K. Scott Oliphint, 2nd ed. (P&R, 2016), 68.

6. Although some among the eleven disciples hesitated yet also worshiped when they saw the risen Jesus, further experiences with Jesus, communion with one another, shared retellings of events, shared prayer, and the inner witness of the Holy Spirit transformed their internal narratives and intellectual schematizations such that these same individuals boldly proclaimed Jesus crucified, risen, and ascended in fulfillment of Old Testament prophecies on the day of Pentecost. See John Nolland, *The Gospel of Matthew* (Eerdmans, 2005) on Matt 28:17.

When we're considering centuries-old miracles described in ancient texts, intervening acts of interpretation are even more significant. Revelation is always "historically and psychologically 'mediated.'"[7] Phenomena such as the resurrection of Jesus are mediated not only through the perceptive processes of the witnesses but also through written texts. We come to these textual records as human beings embedded in particular communities and shaped by lifetimes of hopes, fears, and preexisting faith commitments. All these factors and many more influence whether the documentation of a particular miracle or fulfilled prophecy seems believable.

I've witnessed this challenge firsthand in dozens of conversations with skeptical college students who brush aside evidence for the resurrection of Jesus by appealing to Carl Sagan's maxim, "Extraordinary claims require extraordinary evidence."[8] No matter how much evidence some of these students receive, it never reaches the level demanded by their definition of "extraordinary evidence." When I've asked some of them what evidence would qualify as "extraordinary" in their minds, many have responded by demanding standards of evidence that no actual text or artifact from the ancient world could possibly reach. One young man said he would require a notarized letter from a first-century Roman historian who had seen Jesus alive but who still refused to believe in the resurrection. Another student admitted that nothing less than a personal appearance of the resurrected Jesus in her dormitory room would satisfy her.

The dilemma with which these students are dealing isn't a lack of evidence. The problem is a set of preexisting commitments to a worldview that practically precludes evidence for the resurrection, even if the students claim they would be open to such evidence. Their defective worldview distorts the hermeneutical processes that take place between the provision of evidence and their apprehension of its truth. In addition to all these issues, epistemic defects arising from the noetic effects of humanity's fall into sin are at work in them as well.[9] And that's why, at some point, every apologist must deal with the underlying hermeneutical and epistemological issues that cause evidences for miracles and fulfilled prophecies to seem unbelievable.

---

7. Herman Bavinck, *Philosophy of Revelation*, ed. Cory Brock and N. Gray Sutanto (Hendrickson, 2018), 61.

8. This statement is popularly known as "Sagan's Saw." For an analysis of the logical flaws in Sagan's Saw, see Michael Licona, *The Resurrection of Jesus: A New Historiographical Approach* (InterVarsity, 2010), 194–97.

9. For a historical survey of Christian thinking on the noetic effects of the fall, see Stephen Moroney, *The Noetic Effects of Sin* (Lexington Books, 2000).

In many cases, the care and consistency that a non-Christian witnesses in a church is one of the means through which the Holy Spirit works to make the truth believable. Thus the moral life of the church has a vital role to play in dismantling defective epistemologies. Faithful partnership with the Spirit requires us not only to present evidences but also to dismantle the interpretative filters that cripple an individual's capacity to cognize the truths to which miraculous evidences point.

I suspect that the next time Sean McDowell and I get together, we might find few practical differences between us on this point. Then again, it may be that what I'm describing constitutes an additional step beyond the single step that evidential apologists take from the miracles of Scripture to the truth of Christianity. Either way, clarifying this intervening hermeneutical process will result in a stronger evidential apologetic.

3

Presuppositional Apologetics

James N. Anderson

Apologetics is commonly defined as *the rational defense of the Christian faith*.[1] The five contributors to this volume agree that apologetics has a biblical mandate and is an indispensable element of Christian witness and discipleship. The question under debate is not *whether* to engage in apologetics but *how* to do so. I have been invited to represent the approach to apologetics known as presuppositionalism. That's hardly the loveliest of labels, but it's the one that has stuck, and at least it has the virtue of indicating an approach that focuses attention on the conflicting *presuppositions* of the believer and the unbeliever.[2] Presuppositionalism is most associated with the Reformed philosopher-theologian Cornelius Van Til, but it was developed and defended more recently by figures such as John Frame, William Edgar, Greg Bahnsen, and K. Scott Oliphint.[3] It has fallen to me, however,

1. C. Stephen Evans, *Pocket Dictionary of Apologetics and Philosophy of Religion* (InterVarsity Press, 2002), 12.

2. Some presuppositionalists have adopted the alternative label "covenantal apologetics" to underscore its theological underpinnings.

3. Cornelius Van Til, *Christian Apologetics*, ed. William Edgar, 2nd ed. (P&R, 2003); Cornelius Van Til, *The Defense of the Faith*, ed. K. Scott Oliphint, 4th ed. (P&R, 2008); John Frame, *Apologetics: A Justification of Christian Belief*, ed. Joseph Torres (P&R, 2015); John Frame, "Presuppositional Apologetics," in *Five Views on Apologetics*, 207–31; Greg Bahnsen, *Van Til's Apologetic: Readings and Analysis* (P&R, 1998); William Edgar, "Without Apology," *Westminster Theological Journal* 58 (1996): 17–27; and K. Scott Oliphint, *Covenantal Apologetics: Principles and Practice in Defense of Our Faith* (Crossway, 2013). I should note that Van Til took himself to be merely "standing on the shoulders of giants," drawing out the implications of insights from thinkers such as Augustine, John Calvin, Abraham Kuyper, B. B. Warfield, and Herman Bavinck. Van Til's understanding of the role of presuppositions also stands in continuity with the notion of *principia* (fundamental principles) found in earlier Protestant scholastic theologians such as Francis Turretin, Gisbertus Voetius, and Petrus van Mastricht.

to offer a summation of the approach and a basic defense of its distinctive convictions, principles, and strategies.

A Definition of Presuppositional Apologetics

In a nutshell, presuppositionalism is an approach to apologetics that holds that the fundamental disagreement between Christians and non-Christians lies not at the level of empirical facts or evidences, but rather at the level of competing presuppositions about *ultimate reality* (metaphysics) and *ultimate authority* (epistemology and ethics). A "presupposition" can be thought of as a foundational *a priori* assumption that governs and guides the evaluation of truth-claims, the revision of beliefs, and the interpretation of experiences. The core strategy of the presuppositionalist is (1) to identify and expose the unbeliever's anti-Christian presuppositions, (2) to contrast them directly with the believer's Christian presuppositions, (3) to argue that only Christian presuppositions can account for our ability to make rational sense of the world, and (4) to show that the unbeliever's presuppositions are self-defeating in this sense: If they *were* true, then human knowledge, rational thought, and intelligible experience would be impossible.[4] This is not the *only* strategy a presuppositionalist would use, but it underscores the conviction that a truly faithful and fruitful Christian apologetic must engage with unbelief at the level of ultimate presuppositions. Presuppositional apologetics cannot be reduced to a formulaic method or argument that follows a specific series of steps. It is better understood as a set of foundational principles and strategies that serve as a governing framework for defending the faith.

PRESUPPOSITIONAL APOLOGETICS
Apologetics method holding that the fundamental disagreement between Christians and non-Christians lies not at the level of empirical facts or evidences, but rather at the level of competing presuppositions about ultimate reality and ultimate authority.

Fleshing out matters further, presuppositionalists typically hold the following convictions:

1. Everyone has presuppositions (whether recognized or not) that shape and direct their thinking about the world and their experiences of it.

4. In this essay, I adopt the terminology of "believers" and "unbelievers" because these are the primary designations for Christians and non-Christians in the New Testament. "Unbeliever" implies not merely failure to believe Christianity but also believing what is *contrary* to Christianity.

These presuppositions will influence how a person evaluates truth-claims, draws inferences, and interprets observations. They function as baselines for judging what is true, possible, plausible, probable, rational, normal, valuable, desirable, and so forth. Put simply, everyone has a *worldview* that serves as the lens through which they see the world and try to make sense of their experiences of it.

2. A person's presuppositions will include—explicitly or implicitly—basic assumptions about *epistemic authorities*: the proper sources of knowledge and the proper criteria for determining what is true and reasonable.[5]
3. A person's presuppositions will never be religiously neutral in the sense that they are neither pro-Christian nor anti-Christian. In practice, no worldview can be indifferent with respect to such fundamental matters as whether God exists, what God is like, how we relate to God, how God has revealed himself to us, and so forth. A worldview that does not *affirm* Christian presuppositions is implicitly *anti*-Christian.[6]
4. Following from the first three points: There is no worldview-neutral standpoint for reasoning about the world and our experiences of it. There is no "presuppositionless" stance one can adopt to reason in a "neutral" way about God, the universe, ourselves, or anything else. Our interpretation of facts and evaluation of truth-claims will always be conducted—self-consciously or not—from the standpoint of *some* worldview or other.
5. There is a fundamental antithesis between believers and unbelievers, in terms of both their spiritual orientation and their epistemological commitments. Unbelievers are in rebellion against God, they suppress the truth about God, and they do not submit to the authority of Christ and his word. Believers are reconciled to God, they embrace the truth

---

5. These authorities are typically ranked, so that any apparent conflict can be resolved by privileging one authority over another. For example, if on some occasion the deliverances of sense experience seem to contradict the deliverances of reason, one might hold that the latter trumps the former. For the Christian presuppositionalist, Scripture as God's word (when properly interpreted) serves as the highest epistemic authority; see the later discussion of the place of special revelation in a biblical epistemology.

6. One might think that *agnosticism* (withholding judgment on theological matters) is a religiously neutral position, but a moment's reflection shows that to be mistaken. Agnosticism is a *de facto* denial of the clarity and ubiquity of God's self-revelation (see the later discussion of natural revelation). Similar considerations apply to *religious pluralism*, which purports to equally accommodate multiple religious traditions or worldviews.

about God, and they submit to the authority of Christ and his word.[7] Any approach to apologetics that fails to recognize this basic antithesis is misdirected.

6. Consequently, we should not suppose that Christians and non-Christians have the same basic outlook on the world, and the same basic epistemological commitments, but that they merely disagree over certain *facts*, such as whether the Bible is divinely inspired or whether Jesus rose from the dead. Rather, the apologetic situation typically involves *a clash of entire worldviews* and therefore *a conflict over competing epistemologies*.[8]

7. God has sufficiently revealed himself both in the world (natural revelation) and in Scripture (special revelation).[9] The existence and attributes of God are clearly displayed in his creation (Rom 1:19–21), and thus there is no excuse for failing to acknowledge, honor, and give thanks to God for creating and providing for us. At some level, every human has a basic awareness of God and our duties toward him; but in our sinful rebellion, we suppress and distort this "natural" knowledge of God.[10] Apologetics, then, does not so much aim to show skeptics what they don't know as to expose the fact that *they already inescapably know God*, even while they suppress and deny that knowledge.

8. Natural revelation and special revelation (i.e., Scripture) are mutually dependent, complementary, and—since both are *divine* revelation—equally authoritative. However, while natural revelation is sufficient for our condemnation, Scripture uniquely discloses the way of salvation through Jesus Christ. Furthermore, one reason God has provided special revelation is to correct our sinful distortions of natural revelation and to give us a fuller revelation of the one true God. Scripture functions like spectacles through which we can rightly read the "book of nature."[11] For this very reason, we should not separate natural and special revelation in our approach to apologetics.

---

7. While this antithesis may sound extreme at first, it has solid biblical support (as we will see in the next section).

8. For a helpful discussion of this point, see Bahnsen, *Van Til's Apologetic*, 461–81.

9. Natural revelation is also called general revelation, since it is generally available to humankind. In this essay, I've adopted the former term.

10. Strictly speaking, we should say every *sufficiently cognitively mature* human. Qualifications can be made for, e.g., infants and those with profound mental disabilities.

11. John Calvin, *Institutes of the Christian Religion*, ed. John T. McNeill, trans. Ford Lewis Battles (Westminster John Knox Press, 1960), sec. 1.6.1, 1.14.1.

9. Since the Bible is nothing less than God's word, it is *self-attesting* and *self-authenticating*. Scripture testifies to its own authority as the word of God, and there can be no higher authority (e.g., human reason, religious experience, church tradition, secular historical scholarship) by which it is vindicated as God's word.[12]
10. The biblical Christian worldview is an integrated, holistic system of thought. It has an inner coherence such that each part can be properly understood and defended only in light of the whole. Each doctrine illuminates the others. Thus, as Van Til put it, the apologist should aim to defend "Christian theism as a unit," rather than seek to establish some isolated part (e.g., generic monotheism or the bare historical fact of the resurrection) as though it could stand alone.[13] Christianity is a package deal—it's all or nothing—and the apologist should make that apparent to the unbeliever. A contrast must be drawn between the holistic Christian worldview and the unbeliever's worldview, with the aim of showing that only the former can ultimately make sense of the world and our experiences of it.
11. For apologetics to be possible at all, there must be some common ground between believers and unbelievers to serve as a starting point. For the presuppositionalist, however, that common ground should not be understood as *religiously neutral* ground (see points 3–6). Rather, it consists in the objective fact that both believer and unbeliever are creatures made in the image of God, living within God's universe, exposed to God's clear self-revelation, and designed to think "God's thoughts

12. This is not to deny that there are various objective evidences of the divine authorship of Scripture to which we can appeal. Chapter 1 of the *Westminster Confession of Faith* helpfully articulates both points: "4. The authority of the Holy Scripture, for which it ought to be believed, and obeyed, dependeth not upon the testimony of any man, or church; but wholly upon God (who is truth itself) the author thereof: and therefore it is to be received, because it is the Word of God. 5. We may be moved and induced by the testimony of the church to an high and reverent esteem of the Holy Scripture. And the heavenliness of the matter, the efficacy of the doctrine, the majesty of the style, the consent of all the parts, the scope of the whole (which is, to give all glory to God), the full discovery it makes of the only way of man's salvation, the many other incomparable excellencies, and the entire perfection thereof, are arguments whereby it doth abundantly evidence itself to be the Word of God: yet notwithstanding, our full persuasion and assurance of the infallible truth and divine authority thereof, is from the inward work of the Holy Spirit bearing witness by and with the Word in our hearts." For a contemporary exposition of Scripture's self-authentication, see Joel Beeke and Paul Smalley, *Reformed Systematic Theology, Volume 1: Revelation and God* (Crossway, 2019), 335–43.

13. Van Til, *Christian Apologetics*, 17–19, 149.

after him."[14] In reality, the common ground is *Christian* ground, and one goal of the apologist is to show that the unbeliever has been unwittingly (and ironically) standing on Christian ground, even in their *opposition* to Christianity. The unbeliever must rely on "borrowed capital" from the Christian worldview to express and defend their own worldview (by appealing to reason, experience, moral values, science, history, and so on).

12. Precisely because there is no worldview-neutral standpoint for adjudicating between worldviews, the way to vindicate the Christian worldview over against any competing non-Christian worldview is to subject each one to an *internal critique*, on its own terms, to see whether it can account for the very things its proponents rely on in defense of their position: the existence of objective truth and moral values, the laws of logic, the laws of nature, the general reliability of our cognitive faculties, and suchlike. The apologist assumes the unbeliever's worldview for the sake of argument and draws out its absurd and self-defeating implications before inviting the unbeliever to "step inside" the Christian worldview and consider how, unlike their own worldview, it makes sense of the world and accounts for their experiences of it.[15]
13. Presuppositionalists are free to make use of evidences of various kinds (historical, scientific, psychological, sociological, and so on) and should be encouraged to do so.[16] Indeed, since this is God's universe, everything is evidence for biblical theism when properly interpreted. But that final phrase is crucial: *when properly interpreted*. Evidences will be interpreted through the filter of our presuppositions, the lens of our worldview. Thus, while the apologist can and should give attention to the countless confirming evidences for Christianity, those evidences should not be presented as though they can be rightly interpreted apart from the biblical theistic worldview.[17]

---

14. The phrase "thinking God's thoughts after him" is commonly attributed to Johannes Kepler. See Johannes Kepler, "Graz, 9th and 10th of April 1599," in *Johannes Kepler: Life and Letters*, ed. Carola Baumgart (Philosophical Library, 1951), 50.

15. Van Til, *Christian Apologetics*, 129; Cornelius Van Til, *A Christian Theory of Knowledge*, ed. K. Scott Oliphint (Westminster Seminary Press, 2023), 10; Bahnsen, *Van Til's Apologetic*, 482–89.

16. Contrary to a widespread misconception, Van Til was not opposed to the use of evidence in apologetics. See, e.g., Thom Notaro, *Van Til and the Use of Evidence* (Presbyterian & Reformed, 1980).

17. "Every bit of historical investigation, whether it be in the directly Biblical field, archaeology, or in general history, is bound to confirm the truth of the claims of the Christian

In sum, the presuppositionalist aims to engage with the unbeliever not merely at the level of facts and evidences, but at the level of the presuppositional (worldview) commitments that we all inevitably bring to our interpretation of the world, arguing that the Christian worldview alone provides the basis for making sense of the things both believers and unbelievers routinely take for granted.

A Biblical and Theological Defense of Presuppositional Apologetics

So, why be a presuppositionalist? Clearly, there is a lot packed into the points articulated in the previous section, and it isn't possible to provide a comprehensive defense here.[18] I will, however, make the case for some foundational theological and epistemological principles that support the central concerns of the presuppositional approach. While the Bible provides a clear mandate for apologetics, it does not directly address the question of *method* in apologetics. We cannot simply cite chapter and verse to settle the sort of debates represented in this book. Nevertheless, there are numerous biblical teachings that have significant implications for both the theory and the practice of apologetics.

At the risk of oversimplifying a multifaceted debate, I suggest that disputes over apologetic method ultimately boil down to disagreements (whether recognized or not) over *epistemology*: what we know and how we know it, how our beliefs can be rationally justified, how we should reason and evaluate truth-claims, what sources and authorities we should recognize, and so forth. Apologetics is largely concerned with epistemological matters. It offers a rational defense of Christian beliefs; indeed, it seeks to vindicate Christian claims to knowledge (that we can know that there is a God, that the Bible is God's word, that Jesus is the Son of God, and so on). A flawed epistemology will therefore lead to a compromised apologetic methodology.

Apologetics is downstream from epistemology inasmuch as one's approach to apologetics will be (or should be) shaped and directed by one's

position. But I would not talk endlessly about facts and more facts without ever challenging the non-believer's philosophy of fact." Van Til, *The Defense of the Faith*, 257.

18. For a longer defense, see James N. Anderson, "Evangelizing Fallen People: Apologetics and the Doctrine of Sin," *Ruined Sinners to Reclaim: Sin and Depravity in Historical, Biblical, Theological, and Pastoral Perspective*, eds. David Gibson and Jonathan Gibson (Crossway, 2024), 845–78. For other defenses, see the works cited earlier.

theory of knowledge and rationality. Yet epistemology is not the fountainhead; it, too, lies downstream from even more foundational commitments. Our epistemology should be formed in the context of our Christian convictions, and a truly Christian epistemology should be embedded in a broader Christian worldview with its distinctive doctrines of God, creation, humanity, revelation, sin, and salvation. A self-consciously Christian *epistemology* must be informed by a self-consciously Christian *theology*. One immediate implication of this: For the Christian, there cannot be any religiously neutral epistemology. An epistemology informed by a Christian worldview will differ markedly from one informed by a non-Christian worldview. The proper order of reflection, then, should be as follows:

THEOLOGY → EPISTEMOLOGY → APOLOGETICS

Or, more precisely, given that we approach these issues from a stance of Christian conviction:

CHRISTIAN THEOLOGY → CHRISTIAN EPISTEMOLOGY →
CHRISTIAN APOLOGETICS

In my view, one of the virtues of the presuppositional approach is that it recognizes this proper order and seeks to honor it. Presuppositionalism is driven primarily by theological considerations, as opposed to philosophical, cultural, or pragmatic concerns.[19] With this in view, let's turn our attention to some elements of biblical theology that carry significant epistemological implications.[20]

Objectively Clear and Authoritative Natural Revelation

The Bible is unambiguous in its basic doctrine of creation. All things were created from nothing by God alone; they were created good and for God's own glory (Gen 1:1–31; Isa 43:7; Heb 11:3; Rev 4:11). We should therefore

19. I don't mean to suggest there is a sharp distinction between theology and philosophy; clearly there can be overlap between the two disciplines. By "philosophical concerns," I have in mind theories (e.g., of knowledge) drawn from secular philosophy in isolation from Christian theological convictions.

20. Some of the following material has been adapted from Anderson, "Evangelizing Fallen People." I suspect many readers will (correctly) detect an affinity between the points discussed here and the Reformed theological tradition. It is no accident that the presuppositional approach has been adopted and developed primarily by thinkers associated with that tradition.

expect the creation to testify unmistakably to its Creator. It is unthinkable that God would fashion a universe that fails to manifest its origins in his wisdom and power, a cosmos that appears to be self-sufficient and self-contained. Objectively speaking, there is no ambiguity or obscurity when it comes to God's self-revelation in the natural order. God is *not* hidden. On the contrary, "the heavens declare the glory of God" (Ps 19:1–6).

The classic text for the doctrine of natural revelation is Romans 1:18–32. As a premise of the argument that "all have sinned and fall short of the glory of God" (Rom 3:23), Paul asserts that God's existence and attributes "have been clearly perceived, ever since the creation of the world, in the things that have been made" (Rom 1:20). God has not concealed himself from humanity; rather, "What can be known of God is manifest to them, because God has made it manifest to them" (1:19; my translation). People are therefore "without excuse" for failing to acknowledge, honor, and give thanks to God (1:20–21).[21] Although everyone knows at some basic level that there is a Creator who holds them accountable, they suppress the truth in unrighteousness (1:18)—which implies, of course, that they already possess the truth (cf. 1:25).[22] They also possess (to some degree) knowledge of God's moral requirements and the penalty for flouting them (1:28–32).

Paul further develops the latter point in Romans 2:14–15, affirming what theologians have called natural law: moral principles knowable by natural revelation alone, specifically through the conscience. Thus there is an internal as well as an external aspect to natural revelation that renders sinners "without excuse" before God and subject to his righteous judgment.

Lastly, we should note an aspect of natural revelation that is rooted in the doctrine of the *imago Dei* ("image of God"). We alone among God's creatures are made in God's image, uniquely bearing the special stamp of our maker (Gen 1:27). Among all nature, human nature is the element of general revelation that bears witness most powerfully to the Creator of the cosmos. Although the human heart has been corrupted by the fall and is bent toward sin (Gen 3:1–6; 6:5, 11–12; Rom 6:15–23; Col 3:5–10) the *imago Dei* has not been erased, only obscured and suppressed (Gen 9:6; Jas 3:9). This ineradicable aspect of human nature provides a universal point of contact for apologetics.

---

21. The Greek word Paul uses is ἀναπολογήτους (anapologētous); literally, "without an apologetic."

22. For a helpful discussion of different accounts of the "natural knowledge of God," see N. Gray Sutanto, *A Sense of the Divine: The Natural Environment from a Theocentric Perspective* (Cambridge University Press, 2025).

The Noetic Effects of Sin

Scripture is unsparing, even shocking, in its diagnosis of the consequences of humanity's fall into sin. Every faculty, whether intellectual, volitional, emotional, or spiritual, has been corrupted and twisted away from what is true and good and beautiful—which is to say, away from *God*. The apostle Paul is particularly forthright about the epistemic consequences of sin. Romans 1 is significant not only for its robust doctrine of natural revelation, but also for its depiction of how fallen humans respond to that revelation and the effects of sin on how they perceive themselves and the world. Rebellious sinners simply do not approach God's revelation from a neutral, objective, rational stance. The unregenerate "suppress the truth in unrighteousness" (Rom 1:18 NASB). They have become "futile in their thinking" (1:21) and "fools" who—with tragicomic irony—consider themselves "wise" (1:22). God's judgment takes the form of "giving them up" to depraved practices and corrupted thoughts (1:21, 28). A complex psychological dynamic must be acknowledged here: On the one hand, unbelievers cannot eradicate their knowledge of God and his laws; on the other hand, their default setting is one of sinful suppression, intellectual idolatry, and confusion.

The same picture of intellectual rebellion is reflected in Romans 8:5–8. Unlike the "spiritual mind," the "fleshly mind" (i.e., the mind of the unbeliever) is by nature "hostile to God" and *cannot* submit to God's law. Paul's repeated use of the term "mind" (or "mindset") makes clear that he is speaking primarily of the intellect and not merely of the will.[23] An equally grim view of the noetic effects of sin is on display in Ephesians 4:17–19, with unmistakable echoes of Romans 1. The believers in Ephesus are exhorted not to live as the unbelieving Gentiles do, "in the futility of their minds" and "darkened in their understanding." The cognitive afflictions of unbelievers have a double cause: their internal suppression of the truth ("the ignorance that is within them") and their moral and spiritual sclerosis ("their hardness of heart"). The apostle's doctrine of sin is one of *total* depravity.[24]

The opening chapters of Paul's first letter to the Corinthians present a similar assessment of the impact of sin on how unbelievers think about

23. The Greek word is φρόνημα. Douglas Moo renders it as "mind" while Thomas Schreiner opts for "mind-set." See Douglas Moo, *The Epistle to the Romans* (Eerdmans, 1996), 470–71; and Thomas Schreiner, *Romans* (Baker Academic, 1998), 410.

24. One of the distinctive doctrines of Reformed theology, "total depravity" does not mean that fallen people are utterly evil (i.e., as wicked as they possibly could be) but that the effects of the fall are *all encompassing*, corrupting every aspect of human nature and every human faculty.

God's self-revelation in Jesus Christ. The message of the cross is "foolishness" to those who are outside of Christ, even though they consider themselves the "wise" of the world (1 Cor 1:18–21). Only those whose minds have been enlightened by the Spirit can truly understand the things of God (1 Cor 2:11–16).

Before moving on, let us briefly note two implications for epistemology and apologetics. First, appeals to natural revelation, while entirely legitimate, should also consider what the Bible says about the unbeliever's attempts to suppress and evade its force. We see this dynamic, for example, in the efforts of contemporary Darwinists to cast the clear evidence for biological design as an "evolutionary illusion" and even as positive evidence for "the power of natural selection."[25] Second, we should not suppose that unbelievers can adopt a stance of dispassionate, unbiased objectivity when it comes to interpreting or evaluating the evidence for Christianity, nor should we treat unbelievers' intellectual judgments (what they deem possible or reasonable, what comports with their experiences) as the final adjudicator of theological truth.

Necessary, Authoritative, and Self-Attesting Special Revelation

Natural revelation is sufficient for knowledge of God's judgment on humanity, but it does not reveal to us the way of salvation (Rom 10:14–17) and therefore *special* revelation is necessary. Special revelation is typically verbal in nature: God speaks to people (individually or in groups) at various times and by various means; either immediately, as in the case of the words of Christ, the incarnate Son of God, or through intermediaries such as prophets and apostles (Heb 1:1–2; Eph 2:20). For Protestants who affirm the doctrine of *sola scriptura*, the Bible alone is God's word (special revelation) for God's people in the post-apostolic, pre-consummation age.[26]

Scripture testifies to its own divine inspiration and authority. In 2 Timothy 3:16, Paul declares that "all Scripture is breathed out by God."[27] The

25. One infamous specimen: "Natural selection is the blind watchmaker, blind because it does not see ahead, does not plan consequences, has no purpose in view. Yet the living results of natural selection overwhelmingly impress us with the appearance of design as if by a master watchmaker, impress us with the illusion of design and planning." Richard Dawkins, *The Blind Watchmaker: Why the Evidence of Evolution Reveals a Universe Without Design* (Penguin, 1991), 21.

26. Beeke and Smalley, *Reformed Systematic Theology*, vol. 1, 395–457.

27. The Greek word here is θεόπνευστος—literally, "God-breathed." Although the immediate referent of "Scripture" is the Old Testament in this text, the New Testament writings

implication is that Scripture is no less than divine speech—the very words of God—and thus it carries all of the authority of God, which is to say, the highest possible authority.[28] No other source of truth (such as intuition, experience, or oral tradition) is described in the New Testament in equivalent terms, and thus Scripture must be understood as uniquely authoritative.[29] Christ, the apostles, and the New Testament authors routinely refer to the Old Testament Scriptures as "the word of God" and ascribe them divine authority and infallibility.[30] This "word" is understood to be the primary source of divine truth. "Your word is truth," Jesus declares (John 17:17). We should not miss the strength of this simple statement. It is not merely that God's word is *true* (adjective)—something that could be said of merely human words as well—but that it is *truth* (noun). That is to say, God's word has the *very essence* of truth.[31] Given that Scripture is God's word, it serves as the ultimate standard of truth (cf. Isa 8:20). Its veracity is not—and cannot be—subject to critical evaluation by any higher standard or epistemic authority.

For this very reason, Protestants have argued that Scripture must be self-attesting or self-authenticating. On pain of contradiction, God's word must attest to its own authority, rather than appeal to some other authority, for no other reason than that it is *God's* word.[32] Any biblical epistemology worth its salt—and any apologetic methodology based on that epistemology—must accommodate this crucial facet of the Bible's self-testimony.

---

are also characterized (sometimes explicitly, but more often implicitly) as Scripture (e.g., 2 Pet 3:16). See Michael J. Kruger, *Canon Revisited* (Crossway, 2012), 204–10.

28. John Frame, *The Doctrine of the Word of God,* vol. 4 of A Theology of Lordship (P&R, 2010), 163–66; Beeke and Smalley, *Reformed Systematic Theology,* vol. 1, 335–36.

29. It is striking that even the Lord Jesus, despite speaking with his own divine authority, referred and appealed to no authority other than Scripture as the verbal revelation of God. John Wenham, "Christ's View of Scripture," in *Inerrancy*, ed. Norman Geisler (Zondervan, 1979), 3–36.

30. For extensive documentation, see Roger Nicole, "The New Testament Use of the Old Testament," in *Standing Forth: Collected Writings of Roger Nicole* (Christian Focus, 2002), 223–42.

31. Commentators have noted the grammatical parallel with John 1:1: "The Word Was God." The eternal *Logos* has the very essence of God, in the sense that he is fully divine and equal with God. Daniel Wallace, *Greek Grammar Beyond the Basics* (Zondervan, 1996), 266–69.

32. Hebrews 6:13 has often been cited as a proof-text for this point. For a detailed argument, see Robert Cara, "Van Til and the Study of the New Testament: Hebrews 6:13 Related to Self-Attesting Scripture," in *Thinking God's Thoughts After Him*, ed. Bradley Green (Wipf & Stock, 2025).

The Comprehensive Lordship and Authority of Christ

"Jesus is Lord" is the primary confession of the New Testament (Rom 10:9; 1 Cor 8:6; 12:3; Phil 2:11; Eph 4:5). This simple yet world-shaking credo identifies Jesus with the "I AM" of the Old Testament (Exod 3:13–15), affirming his equality with God the Father in his authority over all creation (Matt 11:27; 28:19–20). The lordship and authority of Christ have important epistemological implications regarding how we approach truth-claims in general and Christ's self-attestation in particular.

In his letter to the Colossians, Paul asserts in superlative terms the full deity of Christ and his sovereign authority over the entire creation (Col 1:16–18; 2:9–10). Christ thus holds absolute lordship over all creatures, including all human beings—*whether they acknowledge it.* This lordship extends to the epistemological or intellectual realm. Paul declares that "all the treasures of wisdom and knowledge" are "hidden" in Christ (Col 2:3). Accordingly, the apostle draws a sharp contrast between "philosophy and empty deceit" that is "according to human tradition [and] the elemental spirits of this world," rather than "according to Christ" (2:8). It follows from the lordship of Christ that every human faculty—including every human intellect—ought to be submitted to the authority of Christ. In Paul's mind, there is no middle ground: One is either reasoning under the lordship of Christ or reasoning in rebellion. In another epistle, Paul evinces in forceful terms the task of confronting unbelief: Not only do we "destroy arguments and every lofty opinion raised against the knowledge of God," but we also "take every thought captive to obey Christ" (2 Cor 10:4–5). This vivid metaphor powerfully conveys the lordship of Christ over the *intellectual* realm: the realm of ideas, opinions, arguments, and knowledge.[33]

The Believer-Unbeliever Antithesis

A biblical epistemology should also recognize the fundamental antithesis between Christian thought and non-Christian thought—that is, between believers and unbelievers with respect to their basic intellectual orientation and outlook. As with the noetic effects of sin, this antithesis receives

33. Kuyper's famous statement is apt: "There is not a square inch in the whole domain of our human existence over which Christ, who is Sovereign over all, does not cry: 'Mine!'" Abraham Kuyper, "Sphere Sovereignty," in *Abraham Kuyper: A Centennial Reader*, ed. James D. Bratt (Eerdmans, 1998), 488.

particular emphasis in Paul's Epistles. In the first two chapters of 1 Corinthians, Paul draws a sharp contrast between "the wisdom of God" revealed in Christ and the "wisdom of the world," and correlatively between the "spiritual person" and the "natural person," regarding how they think about God and the gospel. In Paul's mind, there is simply no middle way. There is no neutral ground, no intellectual "demilitarized zone."[34]

Similarly, in Ephesians 4, we find Paul's remarks about the epistemic consequences of human fallenness (4:17–19) coupled with expressions of the believer-unbeliever antithesis. The way of the unregenerate Gentiles (4:17) is contrasted with "the way you learned Christ" (4:20). The "old self," representing "your former manner of life," is set in opposition to "the new self, created after the likeness of God" (4:22–24). This is a categorical difference, not merely one of degree. The same antithetical contrast is displayed in Colossians 2:6–8. Having exhorted his readers to continue to walk under the lordship of Jesus, Paul warns them not to be taken captive by worldly philosophies that are "according to human tradition" rather than "according to Christ." Believers are called to "philosophize" in a consistently *Christian* fashion.

No Neutrality

It should be evident from the preceding points that from a biblical perspective, no human being—whether Christian or non-Christian—can adopt a stance of intellectual or epistemological neutrality with respect to the sort of issues that arise in apologetics (or in any other field of debate or inquiry, for that matter).[35] For the Christian especially, any attempt to adopt a "neutral" stance, or to suggest that others can do so, is a de facto denial of a biblical epistemology. Thus, while we can affirm *common* ground in apologetics, we should reject the notion that it must be *neutral* ground. Instead, the apologist should unashamedly admit their own Christian presuppositions and draw out the anti-Christian presuppositions of the unbeliever, arguing that only the former can make sense of the common ground on which they *both* stand.

---

34. For further discussion of the epistemological implications of 1 Cor 2:6–16, see Richard Gaffin, Jr., "Epistemological Reflections on 1 Corinthians 2:6–16," in *Revelation and Reason: New Essays in Reformed Apologetics*, ed. K. Scott Oliphint and Lane Tipton (P&R, 2007), 13–40.

35. Jesus was abundantly clear that no one can take a neutral or indifferent stance toward him and his claims (Luke 11:23; John 3:18–21).

No Autonomy

The term "autonomous" literally means "self-ruled" or "self-governed," conveying the idea of independence from any higher external authority. It should be clear by now that a biblical epistemology—grounded in the doctrines of God, creation, humanity, revelation, sin, and salvation—excludes the notion that God's creatures are intellectually or epistemologically autonomous. Rather than affirming or accommodating the supposed autonomy of the human intellect, the apologist should renounce such an idea and argue that the *pretended* autonomy of human reason and experience is ultimately self-defeating and destructive of all human knowledge.[36] Unbelievers can know anything whatsoever only because they are made in the image of God, live in God's world, and are exposed to God's revelation and designed to think God's thoughts after him. The apologist stands on the authority of Christ and his word, contending that only such a stance will avoid the intellectual suicide of rebellion against God's truth. As the apostle Peter wrote, we must "set apart" (not set aside!) Christ as Lord in our hearts as we make our defense (1 Pet 3:15).[37]

The Utility of Evidences

Finally, and briefly, we should note that a biblical epistemology endorses the proper use of human reason (when submissive to divine revelation) as well as appeals to empirical evidences (Ps 19:1–6; Luke 1:2; John 20:24–31; Acts 1:3; 14:17; 26:26; 1 John 1:1–3). It is therefore appropriate to argue that cosmic fine-tuning, irreducible biological complexity in living cells, awareness of the moral law, fulfilled prophecies, and the radical transformation of the disciples following the crucifixion (to cite only a few examples) all serve as confirming evidences of the truth of the Christian worldview. Nevertheless,

---

36. It's important to note that presuppositionalists do not decry or seek to minimize the use of reason in apologetics (or more generally). Rather, they emphasize that human reason is limited in its competence and affected by sin and therefore cannot serve as the final court of appeal when it comes to the evaluation of truth-claims, especially those of Christ and Scripture. Presuppositionalists deny the *autonomy* of human reason: the idea that the human intellect can serve as a self-justifying, independent authority for adjudicating truth-claims. Human reason does indeed have epistemic authority, but it is a *subordinate* authority, and that authority derives from its *author* (God). Hence, the presuppositionalist argument that reason itself must rest on God.

37. Epistemologically, we might say that no one can serve two masters (Matt 6:24). If the word of Christ is one's highest epistemic authority, then one's own reason and experience cannot also hold that place.

we must also recognize that such evidences will be persuasive only when viewed through the lens of Christian theistic presuppositions. This underscores, again, that our approach to apologetics must engage at the worldview level, not merely at the level of "evidences" and "facts."[38] As the parable of the rich man and Lazarus (Luke 16:19–31) teaches us, no empirical evidence can add anything to the intrinsic authority of God's word, and even the most extraordinary evidences (such as a dead man returning from the grave!) will be resisted and suppressed by an unbelieving heart.

I've only been able to sketch the broad outlines of a biblical epistemology here, but I trust the reader will be able to discern how it lends support to the presuppositionalist convictions summarized earlier.[39] Perhaps some of my fellow contributors will say, "I agree with all these points, but I'm no presuppositionalist!" If so, then I will gladly welcome them as honorary presuppositionalists and celebrate the fact that we may have more in common than we think, even while we diverge on matters of application.[40] Regardless, I want to affirm that presuppositionalists can (and should) learn and benefit significantly from the insights and resources developed by proponents of other approaches.

Since every school of Christian apologetics aspires to count C. S. Lewis as one of its own, I'll close with two quotes that nicely encapsulate the core convictions of the presuppositionalist. The first comes from Lewis's insightful and provocative essay "God in the Dock":

> The ancient man approached God (or even the gods) as the accused person approaches his judge. For the modern man the roles are reversed. He is the judge: God is in the dock. He is quite a kindly judge: if God should have a reasonable defence for being the god who permits war, poverty, and disease, he is ready to listen to it. The trial may even end in God's acquittal. But the important thing is that Man is on the Bench and God in the Dock.[41]

---

38. "A really fruitful historical apologetic argues that every fact *is* and *must be* such as proves the truth of the Christian theistic position." Van Til, *The Defense of the Faith*, 257.

39. For a fuller treatment of biblical epistemology, see John M. Frame, *The Doctrine of the Knowledge of God* (P&R, 1987).

40. Perhaps, taking a cue from Karl Rahner, we should speak of "anonymous presuppositionalists"!

41. C. S. Lewis, *God in the Dock*, ed. Walter Hooper (Eerdmans, 1970), 244. In a British law court, the judge "sits on the bench" and the defendant "stands in the dock." The only quibble from a presuppositional apologist would be to point out that the *ancient* man, no less than the modern, placed God "in the dock" insofar as he treats his own reason and experience as the final standard of truth.

That is the essence of presuppositionalism: God and his revelation are not subject to judgment and vindication by human reason, functioning as an autonomous, self-justifying authority; on the contrary, the (derivative) authority of human reason rests wholly on God and God's revelation. It is only through the lens of a biblical Christian worldview that we can account for human knowledge and make sense of the world we inhabit. To borrow from Lewis again: "I believe in Christianity as I believe that the Sun has risen, not only because I see it, but because *by it I see everything else*."[42]

Resources for Further Reading About Presuppositional Apologetics

Anderson, James N. *Why Should I Believe Christianity?* Christian Focus, 2016.

Bahnsen, Greg L. *Van Til's Apologetic: Readings and Analysis*. P&R, 1998.

Frame, John M. *Apologetics: A Justification of Christian Belief*. Edited by Joseph E. Torres. P&R, 2015.

Oliphint, K. Scott. *Covenantal Apologetics: Principles and Practice in Defense of Our Faith*. Crossway, 2013.

Van Til, Cornelius. *Christian Apologetics*. Second edition. Edited by William Edgar. P&R, 2003.

42. C. S. Lewis, "Is Theology Poetry?," in *Weight of Glory*, 140 (italics added).

Responses to Presuppositional Apologetics

Classical Apologetics Response

Melissa Cain Travis

The central claim of the presuppositionalist perspective, as characterized by James Anderson, is the idea that "the fundamental disagreement between Christians and non-Christians lies not at the level of empirical facts or evidence but rather at the level of competing presuppositions about *ultimate reality* (metaphysics) and *ultimate authority* (epistemology and ethics)." Therefore, this is the level at which the Christian apologist should engage with non-Christian perspectives. Although it should be acknowledged that many, if not most, nonbelievers have never once thought about the philosophical underpinnings of their worldview—or even the concept of worldview—the fact remains that naturalistic philosophies and nearly all other religious belief systems are intrinsically incoherent.[1]

As Christians, we should all agree with Anderson that God's existence is necessary for humanity to have access to knowledge of any kind. At the same time, it is also obvious that regardless of a person's presuppositions about ultimate reality and epistemological authority, they can attain various kinds of knowledge about the world through rational processes. This is because to reason accurately about *anything at all* is to *participate* (whether knowingly or not) in the divine *Logos*, the paradigm of reason. Our reasoning capacities are designed to be attuned to laws of rationality that ultimately subsist in and flow from God's nature. It is only through this common grace enjoyed by all of humankind that anyone can reason about anything at all. To conclude that three plus two equals five or to draw a correct conclusion

---

1. Perhaps Judaism would be the exception to this pattern of incoherence, but this is not mentioned in the chapter. Arguably, evidence for the reliability of the New Testament and the resurrection of Jesus constitute the only rational approach to the Jewish position, which involves the same key assumptions as Christianity in regard to ultimate reality, human nature, and the grounding of rationality. It might be, however, that this is a point at which presuppositionalism breaks down.

from a body of scientific evidence is to operate according to this common grace, even if one fails to acknowledge the transcendent grounding of rationality. This cognitive faculty of God's image-bearing creatures is the bridge upon which one can meet unbelievers and invite them to reason together (Isa 1:18). In other words, it is only this cognitive faculty that makes apologetics of any kind possible.

Yes, humanity suffers the noetic effects of sin, and unrepentant humanity lives in a state of rebellion against the truths of God (Rom 1:18). Thus, in defense of the presuppositional approach, Anderson surmises that "we should not suppose that unbelievers can adopt a stance of dispassionate, unbiased objectivity when it comes to interpreting and evaluating the evidence for Christianity." Whether or not unbiased objectivity is possible, however, is rendered a moot point if we assume—as we should—that *the Holy Spirit's activity is essential throughout every person's journey to the knowledge of God.* Clearly, the Spirit has often been pleased to use general revelation as a preliminary phase leading to the salvific necessity of the specially revealed gospel. This is an example of the principle that Anderson rightfully highlights when he asserts, "Only those whose minds have been enlightened by the Spirit can truly understand the things of God" (1 Cor 2:10–14). Classical apologists essentially see themselves as standing ready to obediently participate in the Spirit's work whenever and however they are capable, and that includes presenting the evidence of general revelation.

According to Anderson's view, "Scripture functions like spectacles through which we can rightly read the 'book of nature.'" This point is well taken, but this function of Scripture does not exclude the other light by which the book of nature can be properly read: *the Holy Spirit's direct illumination.* Many are the converts (such as those profiled in my chapter) who, based on hallmarks of design in nature, perceived a personal divine intelligence behind the cosmos prior to understanding God's identity or accepting how to be reconciled to God. We should celebrate this wonderful fact and be thankful that we have at our disposal sound apologetics tools with which to equip ourselves to be used by the Spirit in this process.

While Anderson acknowledges the value of evidence from nature and history in terms of confirming the Christian worldview, he argues that "such evidences will only be persuasive when viewed through the lens of Christian theistic presuppositions." One might disagree on the grounds that such evidence may be (and clearly has been) deemed compelling when wielded by an apologist participating alongside the superintending work of the Holy

Spirit. In such instances, perhaps the person is struck by the existence of God or the truth of the gospel in an immediate kind of way.[2]

I now return to the issue of human reason and God, which is central to Anderson's presuppositional view and regarding which the classical apologist and the presuppositionalist may find some commonality. He writes:

> For apologetics to be possible at all, there must be some common ground between believers and unbelievers to serve as a starting point. For the presuppositionalist, however, that common ground should not be understood as *religiously neutral* ground. . . . Rather, it consists in the objective fact that both believer and unbeliever are creatures made in the image of God, living within God's universe, exposed to God's clear self-revelation, and designed "to think God's thoughts after him." In reality, the common ground is *Christian* ground—and one goal of the apologist is to show that the unbeliever has been unwittingly (and ironically) standing on Christian ground, even in their *opposition* to Christianity.

I wholeheartedly concur (and not merely because of his paraphrased quotation of my intellectual hero Johannes Kepler, "thinking God's thoughts after him"!). The holistic classical apologist is happy to utilize arguments from reason when conversationally appropriate. Such arguments, which demonstrate the necessity of God and the fatal problems with naturalism where reason is concerned, are powerfully resonant with Anderson's presuppositionalism.

Evidential Apologetics Response

Sean McDowell

Presuppositional reasoning is an indispensable tool for every apologist.[3] For instance, after I participated in a debate on God and morality at a local college,[4] an atheist philosophy professor asked me how I justify the

2. On this point, the work of the eighteenth-century Christian philosopher Thomas Reid may be helpful.

3. By "presuppositional reasoning," I am referring to an apologetics strategy of challenging atheists (or individuals who hold other nontheistic worldviews) to justify their use of reason and morality from within their own worldview. This kind of strategy can be adopted by any apologist whether they identify as presuppositionalist or not.

4. Sean McDowell vs. James Corbett, "Is God the Best Explanation for Moral Values? A Debate," https://www.youtube.com/watch?v=57KZyFgSiQc&t=4300s.

treatment of slaves in Exodus 21. He agreed to meet me at a local coffeehouse the following week to discuss his question in depth.

Rather than offer a defense of biblical slavery, I framed our discussion this way: "I am happy to discuss Exodus 21 if you can do two things for me. First, give me an adequate naturalistic account of objective moral values and duties. Second, justify human value without God. Since your objection to the Bible assumes that humans have value *and* that we have objective moral duties toward others, can we discuss how these claims are justified within atheism and *then* discuss the biblical treatment of slaves. Is that fair?" He agreed, and we never got to Exodus 21.[5]

In his chapter, James N. Anderson has helpfully laid out the heart of presuppositional apologetics. We share much in common. We agree that all people have presuppositions (a worldview) that directs their thinking and shapes their experience of the world. We agree that these presuppositions contain epistemic assumptions that govern how we process truth.[6] We agree that there is no worldview-neutral place to navigate reality.[7] We agree that epistemology comes before apologetics. And we agree that unbelievers must borrow resources from a theistic worldview (e.g., justification for reason, morality, science, history, and experience) to defend their own worldview.[8]

And yet, unsurprisingly, we also have differences. The beginning of our disagreement can be captured in his claim that "a truly faithful and fruitful Christian apologetic must engage with unbelief at the level of ultimate presuppositions." While a faithful Christian apologetic *can* engage an unbeliever on the level of ultimate presuppositions, there is no good reason to believe that it *must*.

---

5. I do recognize that the question of the morality of slavery can be raised as an *internal* objection against Christianity without the atheist providing a basis for their own moral system. Yet, in this case, this person was asserting that the Bible was morally wrong, not that it was merely internally inconsistent. Thus he was assuming a standpoint from which to judge the Bible as immoral. It is *that* standpoint that requires justification. My point was not to avoid the question, as the issue of the morality of slavery is an important one for apologists to address.

6. For example, I suspect we would agree that someone who holds to David Hume's argument against justified belief in miracles, which excludes testimony as a form of evidence, is not going to be persuaded by testimony of the miraculous unless it can *first* be shown to their satisfaction that Hume's argument is mistaken.

7. We do, however, differ over whether we should be willing to adjust and revise our plausibility structures if we become acquainted with more evidence that is contrary to our starting perspective.

8. Presuppositionalists typically argue that Christianity is distinctly needed to justify these "resources," but I think a general theism is adequate (Judaism, for example, can justify these resources as well). Yet we agree that naturalism is inadequate.

We have three options when presented with conflicting evidence. We can reject it, counter it, or shift our worldview to accommodate it. Sometimes contrary evidence is what moves us to shift our ultimate presuppositions. In fact, this is exactly why the apostles preached the gospel and presented evidence: They hoped their audience would shift their ultimate presuppositions considering the evidence for the resurrection of Jesus.

Four further reflections will help elucidate the differences between presuppositionalism and evidentialism.

1. Conflict may not always lie at the level of competing epistemological systems.

Anderson says that disagreement with nonbelievers is not over facts but over "competing epistemologies." Yet there are counterexamples. Some Muslims, for instance, utilize a presuppositional-type epistemology (assuming the Qur'an to be self-authenticating), and many Christians and non-Christians utilize similar epistemic systems (e.g., classical foundationalism). While Christians and non-Christians have different worldview *commitments*, it doesn't seem that the conflict always lies at the level of competing epistemological *systems*.

2. The Bible has authority because it is God's word, but we can only know this by testing it.

According to Anderson, since the Bible is God's word, it is "self-attesting" and "self-authenticating" and thus doesn't need independent demonstration from another authority (e.g., reason, science, experience). Here is where I agree: *If* the Bible is God's word, *then* it contains inherent authority. Yet the question is how we *know* that the Bible is God's word. In other words, the key question is epistemological, not ontological. Muslims say the Qur'an is the divinely revealed word of Allah. Latter-day Saints say the Book of Mormon is a witness of Jesus Christ. To assert that the Bible is self-attesting, and other proclaimed Scriptures are not, is to beg the question. Scripture doesn't espouse self-attestation but offers miracles and fulfilled prophecy for its justification (e.g., Deut 18:21–22; Matt 11:2–6; Acts 17:31). This is why epistemology should come before apologetics and theology. In sum, the Bible has authority if it is God's word (ontology), but we can only know this by testing it (epistemology), which is what Scripture invites us to do.

ONTOLOGY
(from Greek *ontos*, being)
Branch of metaphysics concerned with what is real.

3. The wise apologist weighs doctrines according to how central they are to the faith.

Third, Anderson claims that apologists should defend Christianity as a whole, not isolated parts. In other words, "It's all or nothing." This seems problematic to me.[9] Does he mean that if inerrancy is false, then so is Christianity? This sets the bar incredibly low for the skeptic and incredibly high for the believer. Should the possibility of a single error in Scripture, no matter how trivial, be considered as significant as discovering the body of Jesus? An error might make us rethink what it means to say that the Bible is inspired, but finding the body of Jesus would shatter Christianity (1 Cor 15:14, 17). Positively, if Jesus has been resurrected, then he is divine (Rom 1:3–4). Rather than defending all doctrines equivalently, the wise apologist weighs them according to how central they are to the faith.

4. Presentation of evidence cannot be separated from the work of the Holy Spirit.

Finally, in the section on the noetic effects of sin, Anderson writes, "Only those whose minds have been enlightened by the Spirit can truly understand the things of God." I agree! Yet it is important to emphasize that evidentialists (and really *all* apologists) do not believe the presentation of evidence can be separated from the work of the Holy Spirit. We are called to preach the gospel *and* to present evidence, while trusting that the Holy Spirit is the one who works in people's hearts. God is the one who changes minds. Our job is to be faithful.

Cultural Apologetics Response to Presuppositional Apologetics

D.A. Horton

The harmony between James N. Anderson's explanation of the presuppositional apologetic method and cultural apologetics resonated well with the hip-hop part of my being. I appreciate deep and profound lyrics delivered

9. Interestingly, the transcendental argument, a favorite among presuppositionalists, does not defend Christianity as a whole unit.

in a cadence that complements a head-bobbing instrumental. Part of the rhythm of my life as a missiologist is the pursuit of common ground that is religious, not neutral; Anderson's words provided deep and profound lyrics that matched the cadence of this missiologist's cultural apologetic. Anderson's assertion that "the unbeliever must rely on 'borrowed capital' from the Christian worldview to express and defend his own worldview" provides a significant segue for evangelistic conversations, recognizing the Christian worldview as the system that the inquirer or skeptic draws from.

Cultural apologetics is most effectively pursued by understanding the presuppositions of non-Jesus followers by demonstrating how sin has distorted their path to an accurate God-glorifying conclusion, and then redirecting their focus to the comprehensive and authoritative lordship of Jesus. While reading Anderson's contribution, I found myself taking notes as one sitting under his instruction. A few points I'd like to offer are as follows:

- All conversations with people who hold to a non-Christian worldview should be considered qualitative data, albeit not in a way that leads the Jesus follower to reduce people to research projects. Instead, intercessory prayers can be offered during conversations, whereas the conversations may be considered, summarized, and documented afterward. This equips us with not only an archive of recorded data but also—as Anderson suggests—the tools for "an internal critique" of the non-Christian worldview, using its own terminology alongside quotations from its own adherents.
- In marginalized communities existing off the beaten path of the academy, conversations often gravitate toward the realms of life interpreted through paradigms of mystery, superstition, and the supernatural. The beliefs and values of such adherents are certainly not religiously neutral. The task for the follower of Christ is to connect their existing beliefs to the Christian worldview, to pinpoint the idolatries in their beliefs, and then to redirect them toward a clearly defined and reliable pathway to Jesus.
- Since there is no neutral view of Christ, I must be diligent to remain dependent on the Holy Spirit to allow the lens through which I view non-Jesus followers to be a lens that is colored by compassion. The god of this age has blinded them from seeing the light of the gospel, which proclaims the glory of Jesus (2 Cor 4:4).

Ecclesial Apologetics Response

Timothy Paul Jones

For each day of classes I took when pursuing my Master of Divinity degree, I spent four hours in the car, traveling back and forth between my seminary and the small town where I served as pastor. During my first semester, someone gave me a case of cassette tapes with forty hours of R.C. Sproul's recorded lectures on philosophy and classical apologetics. During those three years of driving to and from seminary, I replayed that set of lectures until the cassettes wore out. Three decades later, Sproul's gravelly explanations of philosophical concepts still shape much of what I say when I teach the history of apologetics.

Despite listening to R.C. Sproul's defenses of the classical arguments more times than I can recall, I never did embrace his case for two-step classical apologetics. What I did assimilate from Sproul, however, was a firm conviction that presuppositional apologetics is irrational and fideistic.[10] My initial reading of Cornelius Van Til's works created more confusion than clarity in my mind, which only served to confirm my initial negative assessment of presuppositionalism. As a result, my focus turned toward evidential apologetics and the historical reliability of the Gospels.

In the years that followed, evangelistic encounters with college students revealed weaknesses in my evidential approach. In particular, I saw that no amount of evidence could satisfy some of these students because their pretheoretical commitments had already ruled out every conclusion for which I was providing evidence. As I reflected on these challenges, I returned to the works of Francis Schaeffer around the same time that the first volumes of Herman Bavinck's *Reformed Dogmatics* began to be released in English. One result of these readings was a recognition that I had been operating with a defective understanding of presuppositional thinking and worldview apologetics. Regardless of whether presuppositionalism is the best apologetics method, presuppositional approaches are neither irrational nor fideistic, and the streams of apologetics represented by Cornelius Van Til and

10. For Sproul's perspective on presuppositional apologetics, see, e.g., R.C. Sproul et al., *Classical Apologetics* (Zondervan, 1984), 183–240. Despite being convinced that Van Til's presuppositionalist approach undermines Christian apologetics, Sproul always spoke about Cornelius Van Til himself with the deepest respect. Even in my personal interactions with Sproul in the decade before his passing, I never once heard him speak any negative or disparaging word about Van Til himself.

Gordon Clark has far more to offer than I recognized during those years of driving back and forth to seminary.

James N. Anderson's chapter portrays an apologetics method that I would describe as "mere presuppositionalism"—a Reformed approach that would be as recognizable to Bavinck as to Van Til. By focusing on mere presuppositionalism, Anderson's chapter sidesteps the idiosyncrasies and overstatements that sometimes characterized Van Til's thought.[11] The result is a robust case for the validity and vitality of presuppositional apologetics.

I do not protest mere presuppositionalism as it is presented in this chapter. At the same time, I'm not uncritical of certain aspects of presuppositionalism. And so, my goal is to respond to this chapter with a couple of questions that might serve to strengthen presuppositional approaches.

1. Does presuppositional apologetics adequately recognize that some Christian commitments are more central than others?

Defenders of presuppositionalism rightly emphasize the necessity of a coherent Christian worldview but sometimes seem to treat every component of a Reformed Christian worldview as equally crucial without recognizing that some aspects are more central than others.[12] A Christian view of life and the world certainly requires belief in the Bible. And yet, a Christian worldview must encompass more than mere confidence in Scripture. If bare belief in the Bible were sufficient, then Jehovah's Witnesses and some other cults would survive the cut. A Christian worldview entails orthodox convictions not only about Scripture but also about God, creation, humanity, sin, and salvation. Even here, however, the precise perimeter of a Christian worldview might not be clear-cut. For example, Anderson and I might agree that C. S. Lewis practiced a Christian worldview. At the same time, both of

11. One example of such an overclaim might be Cornelius Van Til's contention that the ontological Trinity exclusively solves the perennial philosophical problem of the One and the Many and thus that the truth of the Triune God of Scripture may be proven using a transcendental argument based on any act of rational predication. See chap. 16 in Van Til, *A Survey of Christian Epistemology*, vol. 2 in *In Defense of the Faith* (Presbyterian & Reformed, 1969). See also Van Til, *An Introduction to Systematic Theology*, ed. William Edgar, 2nd ed. (P&R, 2007), 59, 363; and Van Til, *The Defense of the Faith*, ed. K. Scott Oliphint, 4th ed. (P&R, 2008), 227–35, 395–98.

12. Van Til did—to his credit—clearly define what he believed to be necessary for a coherent worldview, which consisted of confessional Calvinism that holds no fundamentals in common with other Christians. See Van Til, "My Credo," in *Jerusalem and Athens*, ed. E. R. Geehan, repr. ed. (P&R, 2023), 15. Later presuppositionalists have tended to practice a broader, but also less clear, approach to what Christian worldview requires.

us would also recognize serious defects in Lewis's view of Scripture, which did not include a belief in inerrancy.[13]

When it comes to what a Christian worldview requires, one aspect of the answer to this dilemma is to admit that no one—not even the most faithful Christian—practices a completely consistent worldview.[14] Our epistemological habits are afflicted not only by the noetic effects of the fall but also by hidden abscesses of rebellion and doubt of which we may not be fully aware. Another aspect of the answer might be to recognize that some commitments in a Christian worldview are more central than others, which brings me to a point of possible challenge in the practice of presuppositional apologetics: *At times, the presuppositional focus on defending Christianity as a single coherent whole seems to flatten out the relative importance of different components of a Christian view of life and the world.*[15]

NOETIC EFFECTS OF THE FALL
(from Greek *noētikos*, concerning the mind)
Impact of the sin of Adam and Eve on humanity's capacity to reason rightly.

---

13. For C. S. Lewis's views on the nature of Scripture, see, e.g., "To Corbin Scott Carnell" (May 4, 1953); "To Janet Wise," (May 10, 1955); and "To Clyde S. Kilby" (July 5, 1959), in *The Collected Letters of C. S. Lewis*, vol. 3, ed. Walter Hooper (HarperCollins, 2007).

14. Hence, Herman Bavinck was right to emphasize the antithesis as "a conflict of principles, not of persons or of organizations. [Bavinck] therefore cannot follow Kuyper in concluding from two kinds of principles to two kinds of people and two kinds of science. Bavinck calls that a *metabasis eis allo genos*, a shift to another category." Jacob Klapwijk, "Antithesis and Common Grace," in *Bringing into Captivity Every Thought*, ed. Jacob Klapwijk et al. (University Press of America, 1991), 295–96.

15. See, e.g., Van Til, *Defense of the Faith*, 28–29; and Van Til, *Christian Apologetics*, 17–20. Critiquing historical defenses of the resurrection of Jesus, Van Til suggests that, since no pragmatist philosopher would conclude Jesus is divine based on the resurrection, the apologist should shift to a defense of Christian theism by means of a discussion that begins with Scripture. However, the unregenerate pragmatist philosopher is no more likely to agree with arguments for theism based on Scripture than with the conclusion that Jesus is divine because he was raised from the dead. Why not instead draw from the historical reliability of the Gospels and the resurrection of Jesus to demonstrate the inconsistencies in the pragmatist's worldview, which would maintain a focus on the claims of the gospel and the centrality of the risen Lord Jesus? Ultimately, Van Til did not oppose historical apologetics as long as no attempt was made to present such an apologetic on a neutral basis. See *Defense of the Faith*, 256–57, as well as chap. 12 in Van Til, *An Introduction to Systematic Theology*. However, a presuppositional apologetic in which the apologist adopts the skeptic's worldview for the sake of argument (*Defense of the Faith*, 122–23) would likely look similar in practice to an evidential apologetic in which the apologist attempts to build an argument based on an examination of the same historical phenomena. In both cases, the apologist must meet the non-Christian on the grounds of what the non-Christian is aware that he or she knows, since the non-Christian cannot experience the assurance of the truth of God's word that the Spirit works in the lives of Christians.

Certain tenets of Christianity are more central than others, and the evidences for some doctrines are more accessible to investigation. Centering our apologetics on the most central and accessible tenets of the faith—such as the resurrection of Jesus or the reliability of the New Testament Gospels—does not compromise the coherence of the Christian system of truth. Thinking about the resurrection in particular, a presuppositionalist should be able to build a historical case for the resurrection on the basis of public evidences without compromising biblical epistemology or the holistic coherence of the Christian system, as long as the impact of differing presuppositions is clearly acknowledged.[16] Evidential apologists may rely too heavily on the resurrection of Jesus to prove the entire truth of the Christian faith. In practice, however, some presuppositional apologists may focus too little on this central event by underemphasizing the uniqueness and accessibility of the resurrection as a historical declaration and verification of Christ's claims.

2. To what degree is presuppositionalism a response to the challenges of modernity?

According to Cornelius Van Til, it wasn't until Immanuel Kant's reorientation of philosophy that the epistemological antithesis so central to presuppositionalism became fully recognizable. In Van Til's estimation, the very earliest Christian apologists failed to recognize this antithesis because they assigned a measure of autonomy to humanity; for Van Til, not even Tertullian adequately ridded himself of the stranglehold of Greek ideas.[17] Augustine of Hippo likewise neglected the depth of the antithesis, claimed Cornelius Van Til.[18] John Calvin recognized the antithesis and yet, according to Van Til, still failed to appreciate the full degree of humanity's blindness to the truth.[19] It was only by means of the philosophical revolution effected by Kant that the stage was finally "set for a head-on collision. There is now," Van Til declared, "a clear-cut antithesis between the two positions."[20]

---

16. For an example of an attempt to present evidences for the resurrection and the reliability of Scripture while challenging readers to examine pre-theoretical commitments that shape their epistemologies, see Timothy Paul Jones, *Why Should I Trust the Bible?* (Christian Focus, 2019), 93–99, 109.

17. Van Til, "My Credo," 11–13.

18. See especially chap. 5 in Van Til, *Survey of Christian Epistemology*.

19. Van Til, "My Credo," 14; Van Til, *Introduction to Systematic Theology*, 82.

20. Cornelius Van Til, introduction, in B. B. Warfield, *The Inspiration and Authority of the Bible*, ed. Samuel Craig (P&R, 1948), 23–24.

Personally, I find it difficult to accept that every practitioner of Christian apologetics from the second century to the modern era misfired so miserably until a new glimmer of wisdom dawned, courtesy of categories provided by Kant. That is not, however, my primary point here. What is more significant to me is Van Til's recognition that the presuppositionalist application of the antithesis is a relatively recent phenomenon. Van Til interpreted this to mean that previous apologists had failed to see what suddenly became clear and apparent in the modern era. I wish to propose another possibility: *Perhaps the antithesis, as articulated in presuppositionalism, is not a perennial characteristic of Christian cultural engagement but is instead a result of the clash between the Christian worldview and early modern rationalism and empiricism.*

I am *not* denying that there has always been a basic distinction between those who submit to God's truth and those who suppress the truth (Rom 8:5–8; 2 Cor 6:14; Eph 4:17–19; 5:8). This contrast is as old as the Garden of Eden, and presuppositionalists are right to reject any neutral middle ground between covenant keepers and covenant breakers. And yet, what if the oppugnant antagonism of worldviews described by Van Til took shape, at least in part, in response to the collapse of common epistemological structures and shared metaphysical assumptions in the early modern era?[21] What if, prior to the eighteenth and nineteenth centuries, the social order operated on the basis of a greater measure of "borrowed capital" held in common with the Christian worldview?[22] And, if so, what if the rise of presuppositional apologetics was necessitated by the rapid and radical decline in epistemological "borrowed capital" in early modernity?

This possibility does not diminish the value of presuppositional apologetics. As John Frame has pointed out, even if presuppositionalism is rela-

---

21. For the development of the concept of worldviews in the eighteenth and nineteenth centuries, recognizing particularly the contributions of Wilhelm Dilthey, James Orr, and Abraham Kuyper, see David Naugle, *Worldview* (Eerdmans, 2002), 4–25, 82–97.

22. For "borrowed capital," see Van Til, *Christian Theistic Evidences,* ed. K. Scott Oliphint, 2nd ed. (P&R, 2016), 120. According to Van Til, worldviews would become completely incommensurable *if and only if* the non-Christian were to be wholly consistent in aligning their epistemology with their rejection of God; this only occurs, however, at the level of *principles,* never at the level of *persons.* Individuals and the social orders they inhabit always and unavoidably borrow from the Christian worldview; therefore, worldviews are never completely incommensurable. Despite Van Til's criticisms of Augustine of Hippo, Augustine articulates a similar approach in *De Doctrina Christiana Libri Quatuor* (Attenkover, 1826), 2.18–40.

tively new, it is not on that account false.[23] Presuppositional apologetics could simultaneously be a faithful witness to what Scripture teaches regarding epistemology as well as a method that emerged in response to particular challenges of modernity. Neither possibility negates the other.

In addition to these questions, I do also wonder about the role of the church in presuppositional apologetics. Presuppositionalists are correct to point out that authentic belief in Jesus is a package that's inseparable from submission to the authority of Scripture. That package deal also includes entrance into a faithful community where the word is rightly proclaimed and the sacraments are rightly practiced. [24] This aspect of the package deal seems, however, to have received scant attention in the chapter. Nevertheless, I will end my questions here. It may be that I belong in the category that Anderson happily describes as "honorary presuppositionalist," despite the challenges I have posed.

23. John Frame, "Van Til and the Ligonier Apologetic," *Westminster Theological Journal* 47 (Fall 1985): 281–82.

24. John Calvin, *Institutio Christianae Religionis, Johannis Calvini Opera Selecta*, vol. 5, ed. Peter Barth and Wilhelm Niesel (Kaiser, 1957), 4.1.9.

4

Cultural Apologetics

D.A. Horton

The esteemed architect Louis H. Sullivan expounded on the principle "form ever follows function"[1] and broadened this notion to encompass a universal law. Another way of articulating this simple yet significant statement is that function should dictate form. This suggests that individuals should prioritize the function or intention of their creation when developing an object if they wish to maximize its utility effectively. A good example is the Swiss Army knife, which Karl Elsener conceptualized explicitly for soldiers to use in everything from dining to dismantling their rifles.[2]

Cultural apologetics aligns with this viewpoint by endeavoring to offer a rational justification for Christianity when addressing the reemergence of historical criticisms and the emergence of a wide range of contemporary concerns regarding the beliefs and practices of Christians.[3] Despite rapid changes in cultural forms, the essential function of cultural apologetics remains constant, and the form of our apologetics should be shaped by this function. Douglas and Rhonda Hustedt Jacobsen delineate the influence

---

1. Louis Sullivan, "The Tall Office Building Artistically Considered," *Lippincott's Magazine* 57 (March 1896), 403–9. The complete context of the quote is as follows: "It is the pervading law of all things organic and inorganic, of all things physical and metaphysical, of all things human and all things superhuman, of all true manifestations of the head, of the heart, of the soul, that the life is recognizable in its expression, that form ever follows function. This is the law."

2. Jean-Marie Floch, *Visual Identities*, trans. Alec McHoul and Pierre van Osslelaer (Continuum, 2000), 163–64.

3. The utilization of the term "apologetics" in this chapter is exclusively related to apologetics from a Christian standpoint.

of cultural transitions in American history as a landscape characterized by a dual religious pluriformity. Their analysis juxtaposes all established religions on one side against a merging of nonbelief, religion, spirituality, and individual expressions of syncretism on the other side.[4] Over half of the American population can be classified as adherents of this "religiously mixed" second group.[5]

The latest research conducted by the Public Religion Research Institute revealed several key findings. These include the observation that the "unaffiliated" demographic is the sole major religious group experiencing growth. Furthermore, it was noted that the religiously unaffiliated population is diverse, as evidenced by the differences in the ethnic backgrounds and political affiliations of this group. Additionally, a significant proportion of unaffiliated individuals in the United States are not actively seeking any religious or spiritual community. The study also highlighted a decline in the importance of religion in the lives of Americans, with only 53 percent of respondents in 2023 stating that religion is either the most critical aspect or one of several important aspects in their lives, in contrast to 72 percent of respondents in 2013.[6]

Decline in the American Christian population is expected to persist according to current trends, with projections indicating a reduction of more

---

4. Douglas Jacobsen and Rhonda Hustedt Jacobsen, *No Longer Invisible: Religion in University Education* (Oxford University Press, 2012), 26–30. Jacobsen and Jacobsen delineate the genesis and subsequent standardization of religious pluriformity by discerning the multifaceted transitions occurring in the United States across various domains. Factors in these transitions included the societal unrest of the 1960s that marginalized previously accepted religious and social authorities, alterations in immigration policies that provided followers of Asiatic religions with increased levels of influence, decisions stemming from the Second Vatican Council, a prevalent discourse of culture war between traditionalists and progressives, the evolving nature of religious convictions that departed from traditional standards, and the rise of individuals eschewing religious affiliations and aligning themselves with the nonbelieving or nonreligious under the umbrella term "spiritual." In addition to these cultural shifts, the treatment of religion within American colleges and universities has contributed to religious pluriformity in some significant ways: the rejection of epistemological objectivity and the embrace of multiculturalism, the emergence of professional studies, and a focus on student-centered learning.

5. Tara Isabella Burton, *Strange Rites: New Religions for a Godless World* (Public Affairs, 2022), 18–25. Burton arrived at her estimate through quantitative data concerning three distinct groups that she categorizes as religiously remixed: the Spiritual But Not Religious (SBNR), the Faithful Nones, and the Religious Hybrids. She argues that the SBNR's and the Faithful Nones collectively constitute 18 percent of the American population. When combined with the Religious Hybrids, who account for 21 percent of the American population, these groups represent a total of 57 percent of Americans.

6. The Public Religion Research Institute, "Religious Change in America," March 27, 2024, https://www.prri.org/research/religious-change-in-america/.

than one-third by 2070, to 46 percent of the population.[7] This forecast signifies a notable shift, representing the first instance in United States history in which professed adherents of Christian faith will no longer form the majority of the populace.

This development may bring about a circumstance similar to what Christian communities in the Roman Empire faced from Pentecost through the patristic era. This overview of the religious landscape reveals the need for cultural apologetics and justifies our examination of New Testament and patristic apologetic arguments. The goal of this chapter is to clarify the concept of cultural apologetics and to underscore its historical importance in biblical and patristic literature.

A Definition of Cultural Apologetics

Establishing a definition of cultural apologetics requires three primary elements. The initial two phases entail defining the concepts of "culture" and "apologetics" separately. The ultimate objective is to merge these definitions to formulate a comprehensive definition for "cultural apologetics."

What Is "Culture"?

In the late nineteenth century, British anthropologist Edward Tylor made a groundbreaking proposition regarding culture, suggesting that it encompasses human behaviors across various domains such as arts, beliefs, customs, knowledge, laws, morals, and all other capabilities that individuals acquire as members of society.[8] In complement to Tylor, H. Richard Niebuhr posited that culture requires ongoing human collaboration, since culture is the total process and production of human activity.[9] In both definitions, there is a lack of clear delineation between material and nonmaterial cultural expressions.

Sociologist John J. Macionis approaches his definition of culture—"the values, beliefs, behavior, and material objects that collectively shape the way of life"—by categorizing cultural artifacts into material and

7. Pew Research Center, "Modeling the Future of Religion in America," September 13, 2022, https://www.pewresearch.org/religion/2022/09/13/modeling-the-future-of-religion-in-america/.

8. E. B. Tylor, "On a Method of Investigating the Development of Institutions," *Journal of the Royal Anthropological Institute* (1888): 245–69.

9. H. Richard Niebuhr, *Christ and Culture* (HarperOne, 2001), 32.

nonmaterial categories.[10] Bruce Riley Ashford defines culture as "anything that humans produce when they interact with each other and with God's creation."[11] As presented in this chapter, "culture" encompasses tangible and intangible products (or artifacts) formed through human creativity; these products are transferable and utilized in different facets of society, encompassing both private and public domains as well as within and outside the global church.

What Is "Apologetics"?

Moving to a definition of apologetics, A. B. Bruce conceptualizes the Christian apologetic as "a preparer of the way of faith, an aid to faith against doubts whencesoever arising, especially such as are engendered by philosophy and science."[12] Apologetics plays a crucial role in clarifying for those outside the fold of the global church that Jesus is the sole way to salvation (John 14:6). Additionally, apologetics explores how believers and nonbelievers alike grapple with uncertainties and skepticism regarding faith.

Another theologian adds, "Apologetics is, in the simplest possible terms, the attempt to defend a particular belief or system of beliefs against objections."[13] Alister McGrath defines apologetics as "the area of Christian theology which focuses on the defense of the Christian faith, particularly through the rational justification of Christian belief and doctrines."[14] In this chapter, apologetics will be presented as a discipline that provides rational defenses, explanations, and safeguards for the historic global Christian faith against internal and external criticisms.

What Is "Cultural Apologetics"?

Before proceeding to the final stage of defining "cultural apologetics," it will be helpful to clarify that cultural apologetics integrates components

---

10. John Macionis, *Society*, 6th ed. (Prentice Hall, 2002), 35. Macionis argues that nonmaterial culture includes intangible human creations like altruism and Zen. This process enables the integration of cultural artifacts that have been cultivated through human imagination concerning topics such as religion and spirituality.

11. Bruce Riley Ashford, *Every Square Inch: An Introduction to Cultural Engagement for Christians* (Lexham Press, 2015), 13.

12. Alexander Balmain Bruce, *Apologetics: Christianity Defensively Stated* (T&T Clark, 1895), 34.

13. James Beilby, *Thinking About Christian Apologetics* (IVP Academic, 2011), 11.

14. Alister McGrath, *Christian Theology*, 4th ed. (Blackwell, 2007), 487.

from multiple apologetics methods. As Paul Gould writes, "One can be, for example, a classical apologist, an evidentialist, a cumulative case apologist, a presuppositionalist, or a Reformed epistemologist" and still employ a cultural apologetics approach.[15] While emphasizing the importance of authentic missionary interactions for Christians, Gould identifies cultural apologetics as a method that establishes a Christian voice, conscience, and imagination within a culture so that Christianity is seen as true and satisfying.[16] Collin Hansen envisions cultural apologetics as a methodology aimed at cultivating a longing among non-Christians for the truth of the gospel, nurturing spiritual and moral revitalization within the church to demonstrate the transformative influence of the gospel, exposing the involvement of sin in societal structures, predicting shifts in our cultural milieu, and prompting society to recognize that the fundamental questions of our time are indeed religious.[17]

CULTURAL APOLOGETICS

Dialogical apologetics method that responds to critiques and inquiries about the historical global Christian faith by using cultural expressions and artifacts to redirect human affections from idols to Jesus in collaboration with the Holy Spirit.

The approaches of Gould and Hansen suggest that cultural apologetics involves a continuous exchange between Christians and non-Christians. This highlights the importance of utilizing a dialogical approach[18] that integrates Scripture to address questions raised by individuals who do not follow Christian beliefs. The illustration below provides a visual guide for understanding cultural apologetics in this sense.[19] Viewed in this way, cultural apologetics is a dialogical approach that responds to critiques and inquiries about the historical global Christian faith by using cultural artifacts to redirect human affections from idols to Jesus, in collaboration with the Holy Spirit.

15. Paul Gould, *Cultural Apologetics* (Zondervan, 2019), 21.

16. Gould, *Cultural Apologetics*, 21.

17. Collin Hansen, "What is Cultural Apologetics?," *The Gospel Coalition*, February 15, 2023, https://www.thegospelcoalition.org/article/what-cultural-apologetics/.

18. The proposed framework for a dialogical approach when doing theology in a cultural context is outlined by David Clark, *To Know and Love God* (Crossway, 2003), 113–22.

19. Chart based on Ashford, *Every Square Inch*, 17–19. The three-step approach is outlined as follows: Initially, it entails identifying cultural artifacts that are structurally good, meaning God has enabled all people to make good and valuable contributions; second, it explains how these artifacts are distorted by sin, which steers individuals toward idolatry and distances them from God; and lastly, it employs appeals that are both biblically rooted and culturally comprehensible to redirect individuals' focus from idols toward Jesus.

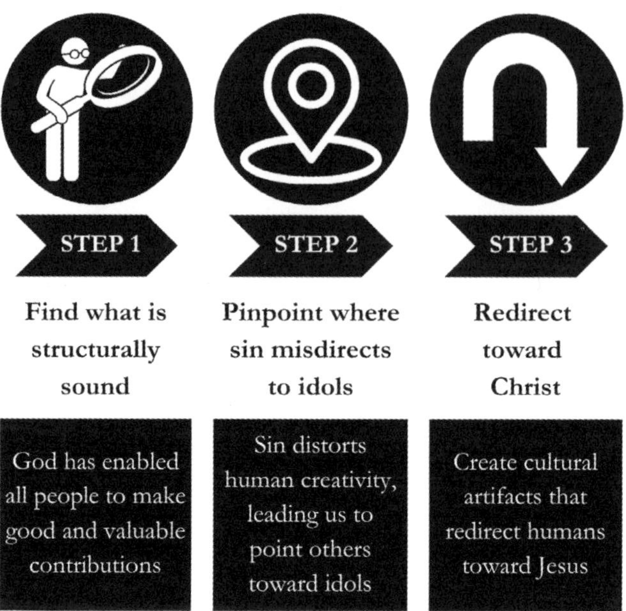

A Biblical and Historical Defense of Cultural Apologetics

While the term "cultural apologetics" may be relatively recent, the definition provided in this chapter can profitably provide a framework for applications of Scripture to culture from Pentecost through the early patristic eras when the global Christian population was marginalized, misunderstood, and subjected to ridicule. The Bible documents the establishment and early stages of the universal church, which enables us to analyze practices of cultural apologetics found in the Scriptures utilizing the three-step approach to culture described above.

In this section, three Christian texts will be analyzed to determine if they support the method described in this chapter. Acts 17:16–34 is a biblical text that will be analyzed in light of the aforementioned cultural apologetic method. John Warwick Montgomery groups apologetics in the Bible into four primary categories: (1) miracles, (2) fulfilled prophecy, (3) natural revelation, and (4) personal experience (what philosophers describe as experiences of "subjective immediacy"),[20] all of which may be observed in Acts.

---

20. John Warwick Montgomery, "A Short History of Apologetics," in *Christian Apologetics: An Anthology of Primary Sources*, ed. Khaldoun Sweis and Chad Meister (Zondervan, 2012), 22.

After an analysis of Acts 17, the practice of cultural apologetics during the patristic era will be considered by looking at *Epistle to Diognetus* and Justin Martyr's *First Apology*. It will be crucial to consider connections between apologetic literature and its cultural context. Robert Grant discusses this relationship, saying,

> Apologetic literature emerges from minority groups that are trying to come to terms with the larger culture within which they live. Apologists do not completely identify themselves with the broader society, but they are not advocates of confrontation or revolution. They address their contemporaries with persuasion, looking for links between the outside world and their own group and thus modifying the development of both. An apologist who finds the link in philosophy or cultural life will lay emphasis on aspects of philosophy or culture that favor his own group's attitudes and ideals and, at the same time, will emphasize a philosophical or cultural analysis or structuring of his group's views. His primary goal is to interpret his own culture—religious, philosophical, or artistic, as the case may be—to the broader group.[21]

The survey of texts analyzed throughout this section correlates with Grant's description of a necessary relationship between apologetics and its broader cultural context.

Cultural Apologetics in Paul's Address in Acts 17

In Acts 17:16–21, Luke's narrative recounts Paul's missionary endeavors in Athens. Paul's evangelistic activities in the marketplace attracted the attention of Epicurean and Stoic philosophers (17:18–19), leading them to bring him to the Areopagus to explain his unfamiliar teachings. Acts 17:22–31 provides Luke's historical record of Paul's address.

1. Find What Is Structurally Good

Paul's opening statement aligns with the first step of identifying cultural artifacts that are structurally good, in the sense that Athenians' intangible cultural artifacts revealed a devout pursuit of religious beliefs and values. Paul's use of a term that could mean "devoutly superstitious" is grounded in his observation of two tangible Athenian cultural artifacts: an altar and an inscription to an unknown God (17:23).[22]

21. Robert M. Grant, *Greek Apologists of the Second Century* (Westminster Press, 1988), 9.
22. The Greek term is δεισιδαιμονεστέρους, from δεισιδαιμονέστερος.

2. Pinpoint Where Sin Misdirects to Idols

In Paul's era, the presence of an altar dedicated to an unknown deity was likely the result of a prevalent cultural notion that misdirected people's worship. This notion suggested that gods unacknowledged through homage might retaliate by punishing humans for their neglect.[23] This widespread worldview entailed the intervention of unseen forces in human affairs; these forces were only occasionally recognizable, seldom predictable, and never entirely controllable. This worldview encouraged individuals to reconcile superstitions by offering sacrifices to unidentified gods.[24]

Paul's strategic use of particular cultural artifacts provides a common ground from which he identifies how these artifacts have been misdirected by sin, leading humans toward idols. By linking the altar dedicated to the unknown god to superstitious beliefs, Paul implies that the Athenians' interest in worshiping an unknown god deserved to be met with an introduction to the only true and living God.

Paul's next step is to pinpoint which specific parts of the Athenian system of beliefs have been misdirected by sin, leading to idolatry. According to Paul,

> The sole deity who made the world and all created things in it, this One[25] is the sole Master of the sky and all things seen in it, and the earth and all things living on it, does not dwell in temples made by the hands of skilled humans. Neither is he in need of help from the hands of humans since he alone gives life and breath to all. He made from one bloodline all the nations of humanity to live on earth and before this he alone determined the time limits on when and where they live, so they all would seek and reach out to feel for him, find him, and know him since he is not far away from all. (Acts 17:24–27; my translation)

Paul corrects a series of specific errors before redirecting his hearers toward the truth of Jesus. According to Paul, the God he preaches created the world and cannot be confined to human structures. Idol worship does not honor this Creator God. The God Paul preaches is also the *sole* Creator, in contrast with the prevalent Athenian pluralism. The Greeks saw divinity in nature, heavens, and humanity, which made it challenging for them to

---

23. Hans-Josef Klauk, *Magic and Paganism in Early Christianity: The World of the Acts of the Apostles,* trans. Brian McNeil (T&T Clark, 2000), 81–83.

24. Robert Garland, *Introducing New Gods: The Politics of Athenian Religion* (Cornell University Press, 1992), 2. See 183n2 for scholarly sources that identify the normalcy of the unknown god cult before and during Paul's lifetime.

25. This is the same sole deity mentioned in Acts 17:24a.

comprehend the concept of an absolute Creator.[26] Paul also challenges Athenian beliefs in racial superiority, asserting that this same God also designed humanity as one race with diverse people groups.[27]

In all of this, Paul recognizes that humans are not "cultureless," and his evangelistic message addresses all aspects of cultural formation.[28] Paul supports his argument with noncanonical quotes that would have resonated with his audience. In Acts 17:28, Paul starts by saying, "For in him we live and we move and we are," the source of which is disputed.[29] Regardless of the source, Paul's logic calls his audience to follow this connection to the God who has a relationship with humanity, at the very least, as the sole Creator of all. Paul follows this quotation with a direct quote from Aratus of Soli's *Phaenomena:* "For we are his offspring." One scholar interprets Paul's use of this quotation from Aratus as *argumentum ad hominem*, since the preceding context of 17:26–28 is not at all in step with Aratus's praise to Zeus.[30]

3. Redirect to Christ

Paul aims to redirect his audience's attention away from Zeus and toward the sovereign God, highlighting the significance of acknowledging God as the source of existence. Paul also underscores the innate human inclination to seek God. This line of thought seems apparent in Acts 17:29–31 when he makes direct connections between his argument and the gospel, introducing the resurrection of Jesus.

Paul's apologetic fit well into John Warwick Montgomery's categories of miracles and fulfilled prophecy, which includes the resurrection of the Messiah (Ps 16:10; Isa 53:5–11). Paul also incorporates natural revelation,

26. John Polhill, *Acts*, The New American Commentary 6 (Holman Reference, 1992), 372.

27. David Peterson, *The Acts of the Apostles* (Eerdmans, 2009), 495–98.

28. Jack Schultz, "Anthropological Considerations of Acts 17," *Lutheran Society for Missiology* 31 (2023): 164–78.

29. The view identifying the Cretan Epimenides as the author derive from a ninth-century Syriac commentary by the Nestorian Isho'dad of Merv in, *The Commentaries of Isho'dad of Merv, Bishop of Hadatha, IV: Acts of the Apostles and Three Catholic Epistles*, ed. and trans. Margaret Dunlop Gibson (Cambridge University Press, 1911). However, in "Paulus und die Stoa," Max Pohlenz calls into question the conclusion of Isho'dad, while highlighting Paul's use of Stoic terminology. Lastly, Peter Colaclides provides a case for Euripides as the rightly attributed author in his article, "Acts 17,28A and Bacchae 506," *Vigiliae Christianae* 27 (1973): 161–64.

30. R. C. H. Lenski, *The Interpretation of the Acts of the Apostles* (Augsburg, 1961), 733.

referring to God as the sole Creator of the cosmos. These realities ratify the legitimacy of his speech as an apologetic defense. In keeping with the three stages of cultural apologetics articulated earlier in this chapter, (1) Paul identifies what is structurally good by acknowledging the Athenians' pursuit of worship, (2) he pinpoints how sin has distorted their understanding, leading to idol worship, and (3) he uses cultural artifacts to redirect their worship from idols to the true and living God.

Moving to a brief survey of apologetic efforts during the patristic era of the global church, this chapter next provides overviews of *Epistle to Diognetus* and Justin Martyr's *First Apology*. Each analysis aims to show that a method similar to the one proposed in this chapter was applied not only in apologetic defenses in the Scriptures but also in the subsequent early patristic era. The Christian worldview was marginalized during these time frames rather than being globally dominant, and thus they may provide a framework for present and future applications in North America and other cultural contexts.

Cultural Apologetics in Epistle to Diognetus

The early second-century *Epistle to Diognetus* addresses specific questions about the Christian faith that originated with someone named Diognetus.[31] F. L. Cross and Elizabeth Livingstone suggest the letter answers three questions: (1) Why paganism and Judaism are unacceptable, (2) why Christians are the soul of the world, and (3) how Christianity is the unique revelation of God for human salvation. Chapter 11 of *Epistle to Diognetus* may be a fragment from some other work.[32] Clayton Jefford outlines the text in the following way: Prologue (1.1–2), on Greeks (2.1–10), on Jews (3.1–4.6), on Christians (5.1–6.10), about God's power (7.11–9.6), about God's plan (10.1–8), and the witness of the world (11.1–12.9).[33]

---

31. Dates are derived from F. L. Cross, *The Early Christian Fathers* (Duckworth, 1960), 5.

32. F. L. Cross and E. A. Livingstone, eds., *The Oxford Dictionary of the Christian Church*, 3rd rev. ed. (Oxford University Press, 2005), 487.

33. Clayton Jefford, *The Epistle to Diognetus (with the Fragment of Quadratus)* (Oxford University Press, 2013), 30–31. Jefford aligns with the consensus of scholarship regarding the final two chapters as distinct from the preceding content of the letter. This analysis will take into consideration the first ten chapters of the letter. For a more thorough treatment, see Henry Meecham, *The Epistle to Diognetus* (Manchester University Press, 1949); and Jeffrey A. D. Weima, "Diognetus, Epistle to," in *Dictionary of the Later New Testament and its Developments*, ed. Ralph Martin and Peter Davids (InterVarsity, 1997), 302–4.

1. Find What Is Structurally Good

When discussing Greek culture, the author of *Epistle to Diognetus* applies a method that aligns with cultural apologetics as presented in this chapter. The author highlights Diognetus's potential to purify himself of preconceived notions about the Christian faith: "Come, then, *having cleansed yourself* from all prejudices possessing your mind" (2.1; emphasis added). This implies the recipient's ability to think critically and to evaluate content fairly.

Looking at the use of this Greek term for cleansing throughout the New Testament, the typical aim of this word is in relation to Christians (Matt 5:8; John 13:10–11; 15:3; Rom 14:20; 1 Tim 1:5; 3:9; 2 Tim 1:3; 2:22; Titus 1:15; Heb 10:22; Jas 1:27; 1 Pet 2:22; Rev 15:6; 19:8, 14).[34] Yet, what about the times when this term is applied to unregenerate persons, who seem to have been the intended audience of the *Epistle to Diognetus*? On two occasions when Jesus rebuked unregenerate Pharisees (Matt 23:25–26; Luke 11:41), his approach was similar to the approach of the author of *Epistle to Diognetus*. In Matthew, Jesus affirms the good of the Pharisees' ceremonial washing before condemning their sinfully misdirected neglect of internal purity. Jesus then commands them to focus first on inward cleansing that would result in the cleanliness of what was external. In Luke, Jesus uses the adjective "clean" to describe how internal cleansing becomes externally evident through pure motives expressed in charitable actions. We have good reason to consider the possibility that the author of *Epistle to Diognetus* used "cleansing" in the same way as Jesus, calling his unregenerate audience to seek something that would only be possible if they humbled themselves inwardly. The author also acknowledges cultural artifacts involving natural metals and artisanal craftsmanship (2.2–3) without ever condemning the materials or the craftsmanship. Following the three-step method outlined earlier, the author first finds what is structurally good in individuals and in visible cultural artifacts.

2. Pinpoint Where Sin Misdirects to Idols

After acknowledging the cultural artifacts, the author pinpoints the misdirection involved in elevating artifacts to the status of idols as well as the insanity of worshiping lifeless artifacts (2.4–5). The author acknowledges

---

34. Other uses include Joseph's wrapping of the body of Jesus in clean linen (Matt 27:59), Paul declaring himself innocent of the rejection of Jesus and of any failure to articulate God's will (Acts 18:6; 20:26), and John describing the purity of the building materials in the city of God (Rev 21:18–21).

the hatred of Greeks toward Christians because Christians do not worship artifacts made by human craftsmen (2.6) before unveiling the absurdity of idolatry (2.7–10). The author closes the discourse to the Greeks and moves on to the distinctions between Jews and Christians. The author opens chapter 3 by noting a distinction between Jewish worship of God and pagan worship of God (3.1), recognizing that Jews do worship the one God in some sense. Yet the author also identifies the sinful misdirection of devout Jews and critiques their rhythms of life, including their sacrificial system (3.3–5), dietary restrictions, superstitious approaches to the Sabbath, pride and identity grounded in circumcision, false fasting, and the celebration of new moons (4.1–5).

3. Redirect to Christ

In the third step of cultural apologetics, the author redirects Diognetus to the truth by presenting a comprehensive defense of the Christian faith, highlighting its unique characteristics in comparison with Greeks and non-Christian Jews. By portraying the Christian faith as inclusive of people from diverse backgrounds and locations, the author emphasizes its universal appeal (5.1–17). Christians are considered essential to the world, serving as the world's moral compass and source of enlightenment. The author describes God as the Creator and sustainer of all creation, including humanity (7.1–5), and the sole Savior (7.6–9.6). The author explains God's complete plan of salvation through Jesus (10.1–8), which provides no warrant for idol worship. Paul Keresztes outlines the *First Apology* as follows: refutation of charges against Christians (2–13), loose summary of Christian doctrine (14–22), illustration of Christ and his teachings (23–60), and explanation of Christian rituals (61–67).

Cultural Apologetics in Justin's First Apology

Writing in the mid-first century AD, Justin Martyr seems to have directed his *First Apology* to Emperor Antoninus Pius, his heir Verissimus, and Lucius the philosopher. Throughout his apology, Justin uses Greek philosophy to convey biblical concepts,[35] following the same process of cultural apologetics as Paul and the author of *Epistle to Diognetus*. The structure of the *First Apology* may be outlined as follows: a bold appeal for justice

35. Edward Smither, *Christian Mission: A Concise, Global History* (Lexham, 2019), 13.

(1–2), a refutation of slanders against Christians (3–12), a statement of the reasonableness of Christian worship (13–20), examples contrasting pagan fables with Jesus (21–22), an apologetic for Jesus (23), contrast of beliefs and cultural actors (24–29), fulfillment of prophetic predictions about Jesus as a central theme (30–53), debunking of demonic mythological imitations (54–58), a discussion of Moses and Plato (59–60), and an explanation of the Christian sacraments (61–67).[36]

1. Find What Is Structurally Good

Edward L. Smither recognizes Justin's use of Greek philosophy to convey biblical concepts.[37] This approach lends further credibility to the method of this chapter since Justin leveraged structurally good immaterial cultural artifacts, Greek philosophy, and the "Roman *biblidion* (court petition)" as tools to highlight the sinful misdirection of the worldview of his audience, delivering his appeal to redirect them toward the truth of Jesus.[38] As summarized by Cross, the *First Apology* defends Christians against false accusations of atheism and immorality from the pagan culture.[39] Ian Shaw understands that Justin aims to correct cultural misrepresentations to stop the unjust persecution of Christians.[40]

Justin's use of *logos* is the focus of the analysis, since this teaching is an immaterial cultural artifact developed through Greek philosophy. He opens chapter 2 in good form by immediately identifying the structurally good virtue of divine reason (*logos*)[41] as Stoics and adherents of Middle Platonism would have understood it.[42] Erwin Goodenough interprets Justin as using *logos* to refer to the pre-incarnate Christ and to describe the incarnate *Logos* as the Christ:[43]

---

36. Leslie Barnard, *St. Justin Martyr: The First and Second Apologies* (Paulist, 1997), 6–9. Paul Keresztes, "The Literary Genre of Justin's First Apology," *Vigiliae Christianae* 19 (1965): 101–2.

37. Smither, *Christian Mission*, 13.

38. Smither, *Christian Mission*, 13.

39. Cross, *The Early Christian Fathers*, 49–50.

40. Ian J. Shaw, *Christianity: The Biography; 2000 Years of Global History* (Zondervan, 2016), 54–55.

41. Columba Cary-Elwes, "Logos," *Life of the Spirit* 2 (1947): 247.

42. For more on nuance regarding the views of *logos* and Stoicism and Middle Platonism argued by Plutarch, see George Karamanolis, "Plutarch," *The Stanford Encyclopedia of Philosophy* (2020), https://plato.stanford.edu/archives/sum2020/entries/plutarch/.

43. Erwin Ramsdell Goodenough, *The Theology of Justin Martyr* (Verlag Frommannsche Buchhandlung, 1923), 139–41.

> The divine *logos* had been in the world since the beginning and those who lived according to reason, whatever their race, were really Christians though they have been thought atheists. . . . On the other hand, those who lived irrationally were the enemies of Christ and so wicked. . . . The Christian belief in Christ as the First-born of God and the universal Judge of humankind is totally justified.[44]

2. Pinpoint Where Sin Misdirects to Idols

In Justin's *First Apology*, Christ is the *Logos* and the only Son of God, and his teaching is the only true religion.[45] D. A. Carson explains John's use of *Logos* in John 1:1 within the context of Old Testament texts:

> God's "Word" in the Old Testament is his powerful self-expression in creation, revelation, and salvation, and the personification of that "Word" makes it suitable for John to apply it as a title to God's ultimate self-disclosure, the person of his own Son. But if the expression would prove richest for Jewish readers, it would also resonate in the minds of some readers with entirely pagan backgrounds. In their case, however, they would soon discover that whatever they had understood the term to mean in the past, the author whose work they were then reading was forcing them into fresh thought.[46]

Although Justin does not mention John's prologue in his apology, the implied connection between them is the Greek Septuagint. R. M. Price links Justin's use of *logos* not to Greek philosophy but to the mention of God's word in the Old Testament, transmitted in the Greek Septuagint and further developed by Jewish biblical commentators such as Philo.[47] John's use of *Logos* differs from Philo, who fell short in realizing the personified deity, as evidenced by his flow of thought between 1:1 and 1:14, where *Logos* is personally incarnated.

3. Redirect to Christ

According to Gerald Borchert, "The meaning of John 1:1 is not merely that the Word has divine characteristics but that the Word participates in the reality called God. That Word was *true deity*, and John wanted there to be

---

44. Barnard, *St. Justin Martyr*, 7–8.

45. Keresztes, "The Literary Genre," 104–5.

46. D. A. Carson, *The Gospel According to John* (Eerdmans, 1991), 116.

47. R. M. Price, "Hellenization and Logos Doctrine in Justin Martyr," *Vigiliae Christianae* 42 (1988): 20.

no doubt about it."[48] Justin makes much the same point throughout his *First Apology*. Justin highlights the concept of *logos* as a sound framework before critiquing the flawed understanding of Greek philosophers. He then steers his audience toward Jesus as the incarnate *Logos*, the one who fulfilled ancient prophecies and the rejection of whom would result in judgment. This aligns with the methodology already described in this chapter.

Conclusion

Over and over, as a critique and in church history, cultural apologetics has provided Christians with an effective tool for defending God's truth. Cultural apologetics relies on the Holy Spirit for regeneration (John 3:3–8; Rom 8) while providing opportunities for continuing dialogue by identifying what is good, pinpointing sinful misdirection, and—most importantly—redirecting people toward Jesus.

Resources for Further Reading About Cultural Apologetics

Ashford, Bruce Riley. *Every Square Inch: An Introduction to Cultural Engagement for Christians.* Lexham Press, 2015.

Gould, Paul M. *Cultural Apologetics: Renewing the Christian Voice, Conscience, and Imagination in a Disenchanted World.* Zondervan, 2019.

Hartman, Dayton, and Walter Strickland. *For God So Loved the World: A Blueprint for Kingdom Diversity.* B&H, 2020.

Lee, Matthew W. *Cultural Contextualization of Apologetics: Exploration and Application of the Apostle Paul's Model.* Wipf & Stock, 2022.

Schaeffer, Francis A. *How Should We Then Live? The Rise and Decline of Western Thought and Culture.* Crossway, 2021.

48. G. L. Borchert, *John 1—11*, vol. 25A (Broadman & Holman, 1996), 104.

Responses to Cultural Apologetics

Classical Apologetics Response

Melissa Cain Travis

D.A. Horton offers an outstanding articulation and defense of cultural apologetics, which he defines as "a dialogical approach that responds to critiques and inquiries about the historical global Christian faith by using cultural artifacts to redirect human affections from idols to Jesus in collaboration with the Holy Spirit." Beginning with the essential emphasis on the role of the Holy Spirit, this approach has much to recommend it. Cultural apologetics capitalizes on the fact that our human experience takes place in cultural contexts that shape our understanding of the world. There are instances in which cultural apologetics may be the most persuasive approach to apologetics. Even when it is not, it is often still helpful. Happily, cultural apologetics is also not in tension with the other methodologies defended in this volume. My only critique—if it even qualifies as a critique—is minor and concerns the *absence* of elements that would have enhanced his defense.

Horton introduces a three-step approach as a framework for cultural apologetics and then skillfully justifies its application using biblical and patristic examples. First, he describes Paul's engagement with the philosophers at the Areopagus in Acts 17, where the apostle uses pagan cultural artifacts to point his listeners toward the truth. Paul identifies what is structurally good (step one), pinpoints where their thinking and actions are misdirected (step two), and then redirects them toward the one true God and the gospel of Christ (step three). In response, some of the philosophers sneered, some were intrigued, and some even believed. This biblical episode indeed exhibits the integrity of the cultural approach as defined by Horton.[1]

Next, using a passage from *Epistle to Diognetus*, Horton illustrates the utility of a cultural approach in evangelizing both pagans and Jews. This

1. Acts 17:27 seems to stand in contrast to the idea that natural revelation cannot function to draw a nonbeliever toward the one true God. To be sure, God can utilize his different modes of revelation, however he sees fit, but this side note is intriguing, nonetheless.

epistle is not canonical, but Horton appropriately points out how it harmonizes with Jesus's tactic in Matthew 23 and Luke 11. This potential applicability in a Jewish context is a strength not characteristic of every methodology. Horton then shows that Justin Martyr's approach, like *Epistle to Diognetus*, aligns well with the three-step strategy of cultural apologetics. This provides compelling historical and biblical support for cultural apologetics.

The case Horton offers for his view, while certainly sufficient, would have benefitted from the inclusion of a scenario in which cultural apologetics is applied as an apologetic against contemporary naturalism. In the provided examples, the target audiences were ancient pagans or Jews who were already open to supernaturalism. Although today there seems to be an upward trend in the numbers of people who identify themselves as mixed and unaffiliated—many of whom fall within the "spiritual but not religious" demographic—there are still many people who are entrenched naturalists with a scientistic epistemology. Alleged conflicts between modern science and Scripture, combined with myths about Christianity's obstruction of scientific progress, are often their main objections to the faith. An example of how a cultural angle could be incorporated into a dialogue with such a person would have been helpful.

As a proponent of holistic classical apologetics (which is quite compatible with Horton's Swiss Army knife analogy!), I regard the cultural strategy as an essential tool with broad applicability and unique advantages. Depending on the situation, the cultural approach may or may not be the best stand-alone of all the options at our disposal, but rare is the occasion in which it is not at least helpful. As cultural apologetics continues to develop, apologists will undoubtedly find new ways to fine-tune and even expand its application.

Evidential Apologetics Response

Sean McDowell

D.A. Horton describes cultural apologetics as the task of defending Christian faith and practice in one's cultural context. This is a helpful way of framing apologetics because various objections have emerged and reemerged throughout the history of the church and Christians do need to effectively address the challenges of their day. Specifically, Horton notes that religious pluralism, secularism, and apathy are growing features of North American culture, and he argues that these trends will likely continue for at least the next few decades. He draws comparisons between the contemporary church and the Christian community of the early church and the patristic era. Based on this comparison and biblical precedents such as Paul's address in Athens (Acts 17:16–34), Horton suggests that cultural apologetics does not rival other Christian apologetics methods but integrates components from each of them.

First, I appreciate his emphasis on how cultural apologetics aims for *persuasion*. One reason apologetics has a bad name today, unfortunately, is because apologists often aim to win arguments rather than to persuade people. While we must make arguments, we should not be argumentative. Focusing on persuasion helps us communicate in an effective and gracious manner.

Second, his focus on finding common ground is helpful. While I differ in my analysis of Acts 17:16–34,[2] I do agree that Paul begins his speech on Mars Hill by building common ground with his audience. Paul recognizes they are worshipers, and he quotes their prophets favorably. Finding common ground is a powerful means of persuasion. It humanizes others, builds bridges, and opens doors for further engagement.[3] Regardless of one's preferred method, every apologist can utilize this approach when interacting with non-Christians.

Third, although I agree with his assessment that there are significant similarities between the challenges facing the contemporary church and those facing Christians in the first few centuries, it would have been helpful to have his insights on how he views the *differences* between these two eras. Given that the *function* of apologetics arguably differs now (social media, video sharing platforms, and so on), should the *form* adapt in any meaningful way? If so, then how? I would have loved to see an analysis of how the practice of doing cultural apologetics today might differ from the early church, even if it still follows the same three-step approach. How would cultural apologetics help with approaching issues like transhumanism? What would it look like to use cultural apologetics when engaging a Muslim? How do we motivate unaffiliated individuals who are not looking for a religious community to care about Jesus, truth, or the big questions of life? And how do we get the attention of people who are deeply distracted by smartphones and social media? I realize space is limited, but these kinds of applications would be helpful for learning and doing cultural apologetics today.

---

2. Sean McDowell, "How to Share Your Faith and Engage Culture" (2023), https://www.youtube.com/watch?v=JWrop6Y509k.

3. I emphasize the importance of common ground and discuss strategies to do it effectively in a book cowritten with Tim Muehlhoff, *End the Stalemate* (Tyndale, 2024).

In the end, given how Horton has laid out the task of the cultural apologist, it seems to blend nicely with an evidential approach. I see no biblical reason why the tools of cultural apologetics cannot be utilized by the evidential apologist, although I would be curious to see how he might blend cultural apologetics with some of the other models. Horton cites the influential evidential apologist John Warwick Montgomery, who categorized instances of apologetics in the Bible into four categories: miracles, fulfilled prophecy, natural revelation, and personal experience. While other passages in Acts ground the reliability of the resurrection accounts in the eyewitness testimony of the apostles (see, e.g., Acts 2:32; 3:15; 5:32), Paul on Mars Hill considers the resurrection to be the divine confirmation (evidence) of his message (Acts 17:16–34). Again, although I differ with Horton in my analysis of Paul's approach in Acts 17, I agree that Paul does make an evidential appeal to the resurrection.

If this insight is correct, then it highlights how cultural apologetics differs from other apologetics methods. What is different about cultural apologetics may be that cultural apologetics is not a stand-alone model. While an evidential apologist can utilize forms of presuppositional reasoning and vice versa, evidential apologetics and presuppositional apologetics are mutually exclusive models. The two methods differ in their exegesis of key passages and in their epistemologies. If cultural apologetics does not in fact rival other Christian apologetics methods, then it might be better considered a *tool* that apologists can use but not a stand-alone model in itself. This does not imply that cultural apologetics has no value—quite the contrary!—but rather that it differs fundamentally from some of the other approaches discussed in this book.

In closing, I want to reiterate the value of cultural apologetics and the model laid out in this chapter. Whether or not apologists tailor their cultural engagement along the exact lines described by Horton, the wise apologist will embrace the larger task of tailoring apologetic efforts to be relevant and effective in each cultural milieu.

Presuppositional Apologetics Response

James N. Anderson

D.A. Horton offers an intriguing and appealing manifesto for cultural apologetics. After defining "culture" and "apologetics" individually, he provides a succinct definition of cultural apologetics: "A dialogical approach that responds to critiques and inquiries about the historical global Christian faith by using cultural artifacts to redirect human affections from idols to Jesus in collaboration with the Holy Spirit." He then gives three concrete examples of the approach: one from the New Testament (Paul's preaching in Athens) and two from the patristic era (*Epistle to Diognetus* and Justin Martyr's *First Apology*).

I have no principled objection to cultural apologetics, as Horton presents it. I'm persuaded that it can be effective in our current cultural moment. Still, I must confess that I have a hard time seeing how it amounts to a distinctive methodology in the same way that, say, classical, evidential, and presuppositional apologetics are distinctive methodologies. Horton concedes as much when he says that "cultural apologetics does not rival other Christian apologetics methods; instead, it integrates components from each of them." It seems to me that cultural apologetics is better understood as a *practical strategy* for engaging curious or skeptical unbelievers. To treat it as a distinctive methodology is rather like suggesting that adopting Robert's Rules for church meetings is a distinctive approach to church government, but one that doesn't compete with *other* approaches such as Congregationalism, Episcopalianism, and Presbyterianism.

At the risk of nitpicking, let me offer a few further points of caution or constructive criticism.

1. The biblical support offered for cultural apologetics as such is slender.

Although Horton cites many Scriptures, the biblical support he offers for cultural apologetics *as such* is rather slender: Paul's example in Acts 17:16–31. Are there other instances or models of cultural apologetics to be found in the Bible that could bolster the case? Perhaps the polemical theology reflected in the Pentateuch and the Prophets, where images and stories associated with pagan deities are appropriated by the biblical writers in order to subvert pagan religion and present Yahweh as the only true God and Savior, serve as further examples of cultural apologetics.[4] In any case, as I argued in my chapter, our methodology for Christian apologetics should be founded on a biblical epistemology, and that requires delving into the

4. See, e.g., John Currid, *Against the Gods: The Polemical Theology of the Old Testament* (Crossway, 2013).

details of what Scripture tells us about divine revelation, human knowledge, reason, evidence, sources of truth, epistemic authorities, the impact of sin on the intellect, and so forth. Horton's biblical case for cultural apologetics seems to sidestep those more fundamental matters.

2. Paul engaged his audience at the worldview level in Acts 17.

I agree that Acts 17 provides an instructive case of cultural apologetics in action. Paul begins with a point of common ground in the religious instincts of the Athenians (although his description of them as "devoutly superstitious" is less than complimentary!). He uses various cultural artifacts—an altar, an inscription, fears about an "unknown" deity, two quotations from pagan writers—either as bridges to connect with his audience or as vehicles for communicating biblical truths. He challenges their sinful distortions of divine revelation and their idolatry, and he redirects them to Christ. That said, I want to suggest that Paul is also doing something even more profound in his sermon at the Areopagus: He is engaging with his audience *at the worldview level.* Paul sets out the basic tenets of a biblical theistic worldview, while also mounting a subtle *internal critique* of their pagan polytheistic worldview. On the one hand, they acknowledge they are "God's offspring," yet they worship deities that are the products of human imagination and handiwork (i.e., the gods are *our* offspring). As D. A. Carson has argued, Paul had to do this to establish the theological framework within which the gospel message is meaningful and relevant:

> [Paul has] constructed a biblical worldview. But he has not done so simply for the pleasure of creating a worldview. In this context he has done so in order to provide a framework in which Jesus himself, not least his death and resurrection, makes sense. Otherwise nothing that Paul wants to say about Jesus will make sense.[5]

In Athens, Paul engaged not only in cultural apologetics but also in *worldview* apologetics. We should do likewise in the "Athens" of our time.

3. Analogies can inadvertently invite distorted views of the gospel.

Analogies drawn from cultural artifacts can be engaging and effective. Still, we must be wary of such analogies being taken too far or inadvertently

---

5. D. A. Carson, "Athens Revisited," in *Telling the Truth: Evangelizing Postmoderns*, ed. D. A. Carson (Zondervan, 2000), 394; see 391–94 for Carson's exposition of this biblical theistic framework.

inviting distorted views of the gospel. I've lost count of the times I've heard a preacher or evangelist comparing Christ's incarnation, atonement, or resurrection to the actions of some DC or Marvel superhero in a way that arguably did more harm than good! I've seen cultural apologetics done extremely effectively; I've also seen it done excruciatingly ineptly. So, count me an enthusiastic supporter of *careful* and *discerning* cultural apologetics.[6]

Ecclesial Apologetics Response

Timothy Paul Jones

Any disagreements I might have with D.A. Horton's presentation of cultural apologetics are pedantic. I'm not convinced that the author of *Epistle to Diognetus* intended "cleansed" (2.1) to be understood in the way that the term is unpacked in this chapter. I wish there had been a greater emphasis on the church as the context for the formation of a distinct culture that exemplifies authentic truth, beauty, and goodness. Yet to critique such quibbles would be to overlook the overarching point of this helpful presentation of cultural apologetics. Thus the goal of my response is not to register any dispute with cultural apologetics. My goal is, instead, to supplement Horton's presentation of cultural apologetics by recognizing some points where the practice might be articulated in a stronger manner, with a focus on what seemed to me to be a significant gap. The lacuna that particularly stood out to me had to do with the lack of emphasis on *narratives* as cultural products and artifacts.

Cultural apologists respond to critiques and inquiries regarding the global Christian faith by working alongside the Holy Spirit to redirect human affections from idols to Jesus by using cultural expressions and artifacts. As a well-trained missiologist, Horton rightly recognizes that cultural expressions and artifacts can be material or nonmaterial, visible or invisible. Some of the most powerful nonmaterial cultural artifacts are, however, the narratives that frame our values and worldviews—and this chapter seemed to overlook the importance of cultural narratives.

Human beings are *homo narrans*, creatures who craft narratives and who are in turn crafted by narratives. In the words of Alasdair MacIntyre, "Man is in his actions and practice, as well as in his fictions, essentially a

6. For the record, I've benefited greatly from the insights and examples of cultural apologetics offered by Tim Keller, Daniel Strange, Ted Turnau, and Christopher Watkin.

story-telling animal."[7] The stories that shape us include not only fictive narratives but also the constitutive accounts that form our national and communal identities.

Ultimately, narrativity creates normativity. The stories narrated by our cultures determine what is considered acceptable in our cultures. And why is it that cultural narratives play such a central role in human identities, norms, and values? Considered from the perspective of a Christian worldview, it's because we have been created in the image of a God who chose to actualize his will in human history as a narrative, and we are all part of his story. This master story started with a perfect cosmos crafted by a sovereign God, followed by a rebellion that plunged God's perfect creation into perversion and privation; it was only through the sacrifice of Christ that this tragedy could be redeemed, and the resurrection of Christ has guaranteed a glorious ending to the story for anyone who submits to Christ as God and king. Every true story in all creation and in all history fits somehow into this master metanarrative. "The whole point of Christianity," N. T. Wright has noted, "is that it offers a story which is the story of the whole world."[8]

METANARRATIVE

Overarching account or interpretation of events and circumstances that provides a pattern or structure for people's beliefs and gives meaning to their experiences.

Because narratives are so central to human culture, effective cultural apologetics must also be narrative apologetics. At its best, cultural apologetics places the metanarrative of Scriptures alongside the narratives of the culture to reveal how every narrative that competes with God's word simultaneously borrows from God's story and yet revolts against this same story.[9] The three-step process proposed in Horton's chapter provides a helpful framework for outlining how the narrative aspect of cultural apologetics might work. And so, in my response, I've sketched out how this framework might apply to cultural narratives.

1. Find what is structurally good in cultural narratives.

Every human narrative includes some shred of truth, goodness, or beauty. Each "splintered fragment of the true light"—no matter how dim or frac-

7. Alasdair MacIntyre, *After Virtue*, 3rd ed. (University of Notre Dame Press, 2007), 216. Even persons operating outside a Christian worldview recognize that "Neverland is our evolutionary niche, our special habitat." Jonathan Gotschall, *The Storytelling Animal: How Stories Make Us Human* (Houghton Mifflin Harcourt, 2012), 177.

8. N. T. Wright, *The New Testament and the People of God* (SPCK, 1992), xxxvi.

9. Alister McGrath, *Narrative Apologetics* (Baker, 2019), 144–46.

tured it may be—will inevitably cohere with the Christian narrative in some way.[10] Yet these splinters of light don't merely cohere with some aspect of the biblical metanarrative. Each connection between cultural narratives and the story of God also unmasks the incoherence and idolatry of every story that defies God's design. What this should shape within the cultural apologist is humble confidence—confidence because the biblical metanarrative does indeed provide a coherent and comprehensive account of the way the world is, yet also humility because God alone completely comprehends this account. The apologist whose life is marked by this humble confidence simultaneously recognizes the world's narratives as incomplete and yet acknowledges every strand of truth, beauty, and goodness that appears in these defective structures.

2. Pinpoint where sin misdirects cultural narratives.

Perhaps the point at which humanity's idolatries are most apparent may be seen in our incessant efforts to subvert God's sovereignty by attempting to explain our existence and experiences without reference to the biblical metanarrative. The cultural apologist pinpoints these idolatries by re-narrating them in a manner that exposes their defects, unmasking how the world's narratives can't even reach their own highest ideals. "The true and the good and the beautiful, which ethical culture means and seeks, can only come to perfection," Herman Bavinck observed, "when the absolute good is at the same time the almighty, divine will."[11]

The unmasking of cultural idolatries is, at least in part, what North African church father Augustine of Hippo was doing with the history of Rome in the first half of *City of God.* Throughout the initial ten books of *City of God,* Augustine re-narrated the stories of Rome's idols and highest ideals. As he did so, he offered a critique from within these narratives, revealing how Rome's allegiances had produced neither earthly nor eternal happiness.[12] Joshua Chatraw has described this process as an "inside-out" apologetic in which Christians "out-narrate" rival stories.[13]

---

10. J. R. R. Tolkien, quoted in Humphrey Carpenter, *The Inklings* (Allen & Unwin, 1985), 43.

11. Bavinck, *Philosophy of Revelation*, 355–56.

12. Joshua Chatraw and Mark Allen, *The Augustine Way: Retrieving a Vision for the Church's Apologetic Witness* (Baker Academic, 2023), 121.

13. Joshua Chatraw, *Telling a Better Story: How to Talk About God in a Skeptical Age* (Zondervan, 2020), 46–50, 62–70. Arguably, Chatraw's approach could be categorized as a

3. Redirect cultural narratives to point to Christ.

In the second half of *City of God* (books 11–22), Augustine demonstrated that only Jesus Christ was able to bring fullness to the fragments of all that was true, beautiful, and good in the narratives of Rome—and that too provides us with a model for cultural apologetics. After unmasking the idolatries of the dominant cultural narratives, contemporary cultural apologists can point to Scripture and highlight how truth, beauty, and goodness are experienced in their fullness in Christ alone. Tim Keller practiced this process through "subversive fulfillment," sabotaging the narratives of secularity by spotlighting the Christian worldview as the sole answer to the perennial dilemmas that drive these narratives.[14] Christopher Watkin corrects the culture's stories and connects them to God's story by "diagonalizing" secular ideals to reveal their incoherence apart from a biblical metanarrative.[15]

As the dominant cultural narratives in our own day shift from neutral perspectives on Christianity to a negative view, the glimmers of common grace in our cultures may grow dimmer and more distorted, but they are never completely absent—and every glister of light, no matter how faint, points to the metanarrative of God. "Every artist is a cannibal, every poet is a thief,"[16] Bono once sang, and U2 spoke more truth through these words than they probably knew. Everything good in every piece of art we produce is pirated from the biblical metanarrative, and every tale worth telling steals its narratival capital from the greater story of God. That's why cultural narratives provide us with some of the most powerful opportunities for cultural apologetics.

---

type of narrative apologetic. For more about "out-narrating," see John Milbank, *Theology and Social Theory* (Blackwell, 2006), 330–31.

14. The phrase "subversive fulfillment" seems to have originated with Hendrik Kraemer, "Continuity or Discontinuity," in *The Authority of Faith* (Oxford University Press, 1939), 5. Daniel Strange applies the term to Keller's approach in his article "For Their Rock Is Not as Our Rock," *Journal of the Evangelical Theological Society* 56 (2013): 394.

15. Christopher Watkin, *Biblical Critical Theory: How the Bible's Unfolding Story Makes Sense of Modern Life and Culture* (Zondervan, 2022), 14–21. This stands in continuity with Augustine's declaration that "all branches of heathen learning include not only superstitious fancies but also liberal instruction which is better adapted to the use of truth." Augustine of Hippo, *De doctrina Christiana Libri Quatuor* (Attenkover, 1826), 2.40.

16. "The Fly," Adam Charles Clayton, David Howell Evans, Larry Mullen Jr., and Paul David Hewson, from U2, *Achtung Baby* (Sony/ATV Music and Universal Music, 1991).

5

Ecclesial Apologetics

Timothy Paul Jones

"It doesn't really matter, does it? Because Islam is going to win."

I was standing beside a book table in front of a London Underground station surrounded by crowds heading to and from public transit. Throughout the morning, a local pastor and I had offered free books to anyone who would take them. Each time someone stopped at the table, we listened to their stories, invited them to church, and looked for opportunities to point them to the gospel. Thus far, our giveaways had triggered conversations with a few Muslims, several atheists, a handful of folks who weren't sure what they believed, and a couple of devotees of Krishna who set up a competing book table around the corner.

It was nearly noon when a British gentleman of African descent paused for a moment at the corner of the table. He mentioned he was a schoolteacher and then asked what we were doing. I told him we were giving away books about Jesus. After chatting with the man for a few minutes, I offered him a brief volume about the resurrection.

"What about you? What do you think about Jesus?" I queried as he considered the cover.

"It doesn't really matter, does it?" he replied without looking up. "Because Islam is going to win."

"That's interesting. What makes you say that?"

"It's obvious, isn't it? Look around you," he said as he waved his hand in the direction of a nineteenth-century steeple that protruded into the sky behind the station. "Hardly anyone goes to church anymore. But Muslims go to mosques, and they have bigger families. Churches are dying; Islam is winning."

As we talked more, it became clear that the man valued universal education and human rights, but his responses to questions about faith kept returning to the same response, no matter what I asked. He wasn't interested in discussing the existence of God or whether any particular practice of faith might be true. As far as he was concerned, it didn't matter which religion people chose. Christianity was simply one more social structure that another system would soon supplant.

"So what do you personally think about Jesus?" I returned to my initial line of questioning. "Muslims say Jesus was a prophet who ascended into the heavens from the cross, but the people who actually knew Jesus said he rose from the dead on the third day. Do you think Jesus really returned from the dead?"

"It doesn't matter whether he rose from the dead if no one believes it, does it?" he responded. "And that's what's going to happen within a couple of decades—no one's going to believe in him anyway."

Since the conversation kept stalling in the same spot, I tried a different direction that considered his expectation of a churchless future. "Which world would you prefer to live in, if you had the choice?" I asked. "A world where pretty much everyone is Muslim? Or a world where there are churches and lots of people following the way of Jesus?"

When the man responded, his words were more thoughtful. "A world where there are lots of Christians, I guess. When Muslims take over, sometimes girls can't even get an education."

"That's been true in some cases," I said, nodding. "Christianity has had its share of failures, but when churches have really followed the way of Jesus, it's brought a lot of good into the world.[1] Think about William Wilberforce and Thomas Clarkson. They worked to end the enslavement of Africans here in Britain, and it was their Christian convictions that drove them to do that."

"Churches have done a lot of education and charity work. They still do," the man conceded before quickly adding, "but maybe Muslims will do that too. That's what religion does."

---

1. One inevitable question in ecclesial apologetics has to do with Christian hypocrisy. Trypho raised this question with Justin in the second century regarding Christians who ate meat offered to idols. Justin acknowledged these individuals' unrepentant sin as an indication they were not Christians and then noted that such sin "causes those of us who are disciples of the true and pure teaching of Jesus Christ to be more faithful and steadfast." See *Dialogus cum Tryphone* 30, in *Iustini Martyris Apologiae pro Christianis. Iustini Martyris Dialogus cum Tryphone* (Walter de Gruyter, 2005).

"Would you be open to considering another possibility?" I asked. "What if there's something unique about Christianity that actually fits with what is good and true? Maybe all the good that has come from the church is only possible because of what Christians believe about Jesus and every person being made in God's image. What if the good that churches have done depends on some reality that's supremely good?"

These questions unfolded into a discussion about how Christians have promoted literacy and finally about how the stories of Jesus shaped the habits of the early church—and that's when the man noticed he was about to miss his connection on the Victoria Line. When he scurried into the Highbury and Islington Station, this individual was still far from convinced, but he left with a book about Jesus clutched in his hand and, hopefully, a hint of truth implanted in his heart.

How the Challenges Have Changed

This man at the Tube station wasn't interested in evidence for God's existence, and he was apathetic when it came to questions related to the resurrection of Jesus.[2]

He's not alone.

In twenty-first-century Western contexts, it has become more and more difficult to defend the historicity of the biblical miracles or the logical necessity of a divine Creator. These conversations haven't become harder because evidence is in short supply; proofs of God are as plentiful as they've ever been. Why, then, have the challenges gotten so challenging?

It's partly because the conditions of secularity have eroded assumptions about knowledge and reality that people once held in common.[3] As a

2. Some aspects of this individual's response are similar to the perspective described by Robert Nash as "apatheism." See Robert Nash, *Religious Pluralism in the Academy: Opening the Dialogue* (Lang, 2001), 27; and Jonathan Rauch, "Let It Be," *Atlantic Monthly*, May 2003, 34–35.

3. For centuries, theologians in Western contexts assumed some degree of common rationality, grounded in an orderly and knowable cosmos, even when no other commonality seemed possible. According to Thomas, it was conceivable in conversations with Muslims "to have recourse to natural reason [*naturalem rationem*], to which all are compelled to assent [*omnes assentire coguntur*]." Thomas Aquinas, *Summa contra gentiles: Books I—II* (Emmaus Academic, 2019), 1.2. The Enlightenment's emphasis on neutral and autonomous reason cut off the modern self from a common rationality that depends on sources and traditions beyond the self. In the same way that no sufficient commonality remains for moral reasoning in the modern era, one might say that the aftermath of the Enlightenment also eroded the common rationality that made classical and evidential arguments convincing and meaningful. See also Alister McGrath, *The Genesis of Doctrine: A Study in the Foundation of Doctrinal Criticism* (Blackwell, 1990), 199.

result, the epistemological substructures necessary to sustain many of the most familiar classical and evidential arguments are contested by diverse ways of knowing, all of which are widely perceived as equally valid.[4] It's also because statements about God are increasingly viewed as relevant only if an individual finds them to be personally meaningful.[5] As a result of these and other cultural shifts, challenges to the church's faith are increasingly less likely to begin with doubts about what is true and more likely to start with questions about what is good.[6] To put it another way, conversations about morality tend to precede debates about metaphysics or the miraculous claims of Scripture. If so, then perhaps that's where our apologetics conversations should begin as well.

I am not downplaying the importance of cultivating a Christian worldview or contending for the inerrancy of Scripture. I've invested decades of my life in defenses of the historical reliability and textual integrity of the New Testament, and I have no plans to curtail this work of demonstrating how the truth of Scripture can be verified. As J. I. Packer commented years ago, "The battle for the Bible must continue as long as unbelieving babble about the Bible continues."[7] My point is that the man at the book table in front of the Highbury and Islington station in London was not a unique or isolated example. A growing number of non-Christians are willing and able to wrestle with the question of whether the church is good for the social order long before they're able to make sense of our arguments for theism or the Trinity or an empty tomb.[8]

In many cases, these individuals perceive the church's moral practices to be far more peculiar than our commitment to an inerrant text or an incarnate God. Some of them view Christianity's moral distinctives as deplorable, while others may celebrate the civic and cultural good that churches

4. Kyle Beshears, *Apatheism: How We Share When They Don't Care* (B&H, 2021), 12.

5. Charles Taylor, *A Secular Age* (Harvard University Press, 2007), 31. When statements about God are perceived as relevant only if the individual perceives them to be meaningful, Christians may find themselves "left standing in a vacant Areopagus with no one to hear our case. . . . It seems impossible to start and sustain a conversation about God without it being terminated by disinterest, undermined by secularism, muted by comfort, or derailed by distraction." Beshears, *Apatheism*, 59.

6. Timothy Paul Jones, "We Are All Apologists Now," *Southern Baptist Journal of Theology* 27 (2023): 111–13.

7. J. I. Packer, "Battling for the Bible," *Regent College Bulletin* 9 (Fall 1979): n.p.

8. Religiously unaffiliated Americans differ in their perceptions of the moral and social benefits of religion. The majority (58 percent) say religion does more harm than good, while a significant minority (22 percent) say that religion is "generally . . . more socially helpful than harmful." Betsy Cooper et al., *Exodus: Why Americans are Leaving Religion—And Why They're Unlikely to Come Back* (PRRI, 2016), 10–13.

have produced.[9] Either way, it's the church's social and ethical impact that's increasingly recognized as the most distinctive feature of our faith. So how should these social shifts shape the ways we practice apologetics? Is it conceivable to find any starting point for conversation amid the chaos of so many contested ways of knowing? If so, where might this common ground be found?

What I wish to do throughout the remainder of this chapter is to suggest a solution that's repeated thousands of times each day during safety briefings on airport runways: "Remember, the exit door you're looking for could be behind you." I contend that the best exit from this challenge to apologetics can be found behind us, in the ancient church. There are significant analogies that link the second century in particular with our own era, especially when it comes to the peculiarity of the Christian way of being in the world. "The second-century world is, in a sense, our world," church historian Carl Trueman declares in his book *The Rise and Triumph of the Modern Self*.[10] Patristics scholars Stephen Presley and John Behr have similarly identified significant parallels between our present cultural moment and the struggles of the second-century church.[11] After considering connections between the second century and our own era, New Testament scholar Michael Kruger has even suggested that what we need today may not be "a new apologetic but perhaps an old one—a second century one."[12]

Or, to put into another way, the exit door that apologists are looking for might be behind us, in the ancient church. By saying this, I am

---

9. For example, a 2019 court decision deplored perspectives representative of traditional Christian sexual ethics as "incompatible with human dignity" and in "conflict with the fundamental rights of others." Yet historian Tom Holland has made the case that human equality and "an inalienable right to life, liberty, and the pursuit of happiness" were never "self-evident truths"; it was Christianity that embedded these values into the social order. In each of these examples, one negative and one positive, the civic and cultural impact of Christian ethics is central. See Iliana Magda, "He Opposed Using Transgender Clients' Pronouns: It Became a Legal Battle," *New York Times*, October 3, 2019, https://www.nytimes.com; Spencer Klavan, "Going Off the Rails," *Claremont Review of Books* (Winter 2020), https://www.claremontreviewofbooks.com; Tom Holland, *Dominion: How the Christian Revolution Remade the World* (Basic, 2019), 400; Tom Holland, "Why I Was Wrong About Christianity," *The New Statesman*, September 14, 2016, https://www.thenewstatesman.com.

10. Carl Trueman, *The Rise and Triumph of the Modern Self: Cultural Amnesia, Expressive Individualism, and the Road to Sexual Revolution* (Crossway, 2020), 454.

11. John Behr, *Irenaeus of Lyons* (Oxford University Press, 2015), 1–2; and Stephen Presley, *Cultural Sanctification: Engaging the World Like the Early Church* (Eerdmans, 2024), 8.

12. Michael Kruger, *Christianity at the Crossroads* (InterVarsity, 2018), 230. See also Gerald Sittser, *Resilient Faith: How the Early Christian Third Way Changed the World* (Brazos, 2019), 15.

not suggesting that the circumstances of the ancient church are precisely parallel to our circumstances today. The cultures of second-century Rome and twenty-first-century Western civilization are far from interchangeable. The vast differences between us and the era of the emperors require not only that we *retrieve* ancient arguments but also that we *reconfigure* these apologetics to bridge the distance between patristic patterns and contemporary praxis.[13]

A Definition of Ecclesial Apologetics

One of the most distinctive features of second- and third-century apologetics had to do with the role of the church in the defense of the faith—which brings me to a practice that's been described as "ecclesial apologetics."[14]

The word *ecclesial* derives from *ekklēsia*, the Greek term that the divinely inspired authors of the New Testament deployed to describe the church. Ecclesial apologetics points to the presence and power of God as the best explanation for the existence and ethics of the church. For the ecclesial apologist, the role of the church in apologetics is not merely to provide a context where members learn to defend their faith; the life of the church itself is a key evidence for the truth of the faith. Viewed from the perspective of ecclesial apologetics, the moral framework enacted through the church's life is impossible apart from the truth of the biblical metanarrative, which itself presupposes a particular set of metaphysical realities and epistemological structures.[15]

ECCLESIAL APOLOGETICS
Ancient apologetics method that points to the presence and power of God as the best explanation for the existence and the ethics of the church.

13. Theological retrieval engages in expectant rereadings of texts from postbiblical Christian traditions with a willingness to critique and recontextualize these teachings; retrieval should not be confused with repristination in which past ideas are uncritically ingeminated in contemporary contexts. For further discussion, see John Webster, "Theologies of Retrieval," in *The Oxford Handbook of Systematic Theology*, ed. John Webster et al. (Oxford University Press, 2009), 584–96.

14. See, e.g., Timothy Paul Jones, "'Something Divine Mingled among Them': Care for the Parentless and the Poor as Ecclesial Apologetic in the Second Century," in *Rich in Good Deeds*, ed. Robert Plummer (Fontes, 2022).

15. For second-century apologists, evidence for the existence of the God of the Christians was inseparable from evidence for the truth and authority of Scripture. After presenting ecclesial and narrative arguments for the truth of Christianity, Aristides points his readers to Scripture: "Take their writings and read them. You will find I have not presented these things on my own authority." Aristides, *Apologia*, 16, in *Aristide: Apologie*, ed. Marie-Joseph

Biblical and Historical Foundations for Ecclesial Apologetics

Although an ecclesial approach to apologetics thrived in the second century AD, the apologists of this era didn't contrive their approach without any precedents. Many aspects of ecclesial apologetics can be traced back to the pages of the New Testament.

Ecclesial Apologetics in the New Testament

Jesus himself predicted in one of his prayers that the oneness of his church would provide the world with evidence that God the Father had sent him (John 17:23). The oneness described in this prayer is a unity of faithfulness and action in response to revelation that results in evidence for the truth of God's revelation in Christ.[16] Three decades or so after Jesus voiced his prayer, Simon Peter prepared the recipients of his first letter to defend their faith in the face of persecution. The apostle's foremost directive was for the church to silence detractors by practicing a distinctive, devoted, and disciplined pattern of life together (1 Pet 1:16; 2:12–15; 4:12–19). The apologetic that Peter called these Christians to provide required the evidence of a community that persisted together in a particular set of habits and responses (1 Pet 3:8–9, 13–15, 16–17; 4:4). And so, it was not only a rational defense of the gospel that would put their persecutors to shame, but it was also the evidence of the church's way of being in the world (1 Pet 3:15–16). The sacrificial sufferings of Jesus were the means by which the people of God were empowered to practice these habits together (1 Pet 3:18; 4:1–2).

Ecclesial Apologetics in the Early Church

How, precisely, did ancient apologists build on these biblical truths to cultivate ecclesial arguments for the truth of the gospel? To understand the patterns that early apologists pursued to make their defenses, let's look at one specific example of ecclesial apologetics in a text penned by a second-century philosopher known as Aristides of Athens.

Pierre et al. (Cerf, 2003). For further discussion of Scripture and identity formation in the *Apology* of Aristides, see Zachary Hedges, "Covenant and Identity Formation in the Second Century" (PhD diss., The Southern Baptist Theological Seminary, 2023), 203–5.

16. D. A. Carson, *The Gospel According to John* (Eerdmans, 1990), 568–69. See also Craig Keener, *The Gospel of John*, repr. ed. (Baker, 2010), 1061.

Aristides of Athens began his defense by appealing first to the beauty of creation and then to an argument from motion.[17] Although Aristides launched his apology with a line of argumentation that later apologists might classify as classical, his uses of aesthetic and cosmological arguments were meant more to provoke a dilemma than to provide an answer. He was not attempting to demonstrate the existence of a generic deity; his goal was instead to declare the inexplicability of the cosmos apart from a particular deity and then to define what ethics would necessarily characterize the lives of people who followed such a God.

Aristides started his summary of the church's way of life with clauses that echo the Jewish Scriptures. According to Aristides, Christians "do not adulterate or fornicate," "they love their neighbors," "they judge with justice," and so on. Many of these ethics would have been, at the very least, recognizable to second-century Romans.[18] Yet this Christian philosopher from Athens didn't stop after mentioning the ethics that would have sounded familiar in his cultural context. He moved onward to ecclesial habits so radical they would have been ridiculed as absurd among many of his neighbors.

Christians, according to Aristides, "rescue orphans from those who abuse them, and they give without grudging to the one who has nothing." Although some philosophers did criticize the widespread practice of abandoning unwanted infants, caring for the fatherless would have seemed ludicrous to many Greeks and Romans.[19] Yet Aristides persisted: "Whenever one of their poor passes from the world, each one according to his ability pays attention and carefully sees to his burial. If anyone from their number is imprisoned or oppressed for the name 'Christ,' all of them provide his needs, and if it is possible for that one to be delivered, they deliver him."[20]

---

17. Aristides of Athens, *Apologia*, 1. The argument from motion may derive in part from Aristotle, "Αριστοτελους των Μετά τα Φυσικά Λ," *Metaphysics, Volume II: Books 10–14. Oeconomica. Magna Moralia* (Harvard University Press, 1935), 12.6–9 (1071b).

18. Justin Martyr similarly began with ethical patterns that might have been acceptable among some philosophically minded Romans before moving to practices that likely would have been rejected or ridiculed. See Justin Martyr, *Apologia A*, chaps. 14–15 in *Apologie pour les Chrétiens*, ed. Charles Munier (Cerf, 2006). For similar patterns in the second-century apology of Theophilus, see Stuart Parsons, *Ancient Apologetic Exegesis: Introducing and Recovering Theophilus's World* (Pickwick, 2015), 110–19. The first-century Stoic Musonius took a negative view of sexual relations outside marriage; see lectures 12 and 13 in Gaius Musonius Rufus, *C. Musonii Rufi*, ed. Otto Hense (Teubner, 1905).

19. O. M. Bakke, *When Children Became People: The Birth of Childhood in Early Christianity*, trans. Brian McNeil (Fortress Press, 2005), 28–33.

20. Aristides, *Apologia*, chap. 15.

These patterns of generosity that shattered social divisions are precisely the habits that second-century satirist Lucian of Samosata mocked when he depicted a Cynic philosopher's short-lived sally into the Christian way of life.[21]

After detailing the church's countercultural ethics, Aristides declared that these practices were precisely the habits that ought to be expected among people who worship the true God. "Truly, this is a new people," Aristides exulted as he considered the church's way of life, "and there is something divine mingled among them."[22] When he claimed God's presence was mingled in the communion of the saints, Aristides was not simply suggesting that the goodness of the church's deeds demonstrated the presence of the divine; unrighteous people are, after all, capable of pursuing philanthropy and promoting righteous laws on the basis of common grace. What Aristides was pointing out was *the impossibility of sustaining such counterintuitive and countercultural habits of life as a community apart from the presence of some power that transcends every human capacity*. This ecclesial apologetic can be classified with arguments identified later in history as "abductive."[23]

Inhabitants of the second- and third-century Roman Empire did not question the church's proclamation because the central dogmas of the Christian faith were supernatural.[24] Christians were distrusted due to

---

21. Lucian of Samosata, "Περί της Περεγρινου Τελευτης," *The Passing of Peregrinus. The Runaways. Toxaris or Friendship. The Dance. Lexiphanes. The Eunuch. Astrology. The Mistaken Critic. The Parliament of the Gods. The Tyrannicide Disowned* (Harvard University Press, 1936), chaps. 11–13, 16.

22. Aristides, *Apologia*, chap. 16, Syriac. Although this clause accurately expresses the overall argument of the *Apologia*, it is possible that this sentence is unique to the Syriac translation and did not appear in the original Greek text.

23. In abductive argumentation, a surprising fact (C) is observed; it is acknowledged that, if proposition A were true, C would be a matter of course; thus it becomes reasonable to suspect that A is true. If A provides the best explanation for C in comparison with other possible explanations, it is reasonable to accept A. See Charles Peirce, "Pragmatism as the Logic of Abduction," *The Essential Peirce (1893–1913): Selected Philosophical Writings* (Indiana University Press, 1998), 231. In the *Apologia* of Aristides, the moral habits of the church are observed as factual, and the reality of the Christian God is presented as the best explanation for this phenomenon. For examples of abductive argumentation in modern and contemporary apologetics, see, e.g., Douglas Groothuis, "Deposed Royalty: Pascal's Anthropological Argument," *Journal of the Evangelical Theological Society* 41 (June 1998): 309–11; Alister McGrath, *The Intellectual World of C. S. Lewis* (Wiley-Blackwell, 2013), 105, 120; Michael Peterson, *C. S. Lewis and the Christian Worldview* (Oxford University Press, 2020), 16; and Gavin Ortlund, *Why God Makes Sense in a World That Doesn't: The Beauty of Christian Theism* (Baker, 2021), 11–13. The argument in Aristides could also, arguably, be classified as "transcendental."

24. Trueman, *Rise and Triumph of the Modern Self*, 454.

their countercultural allegiances and their way of being in the world. The kingship of Jesus sounded subversive, the church's liturgy seemed suspicious, the church's care for the vulnerable was ludicrous, and the sexual morals that marked the lives of Christians struck their neighbors as odd. Charity for the weak and disabled was perceived as a defect to be mocked, not a pattern of life to be praised.

Nevertheless, the absurdities of the church's common life also turned out to be attractive to some inhabitants of the empire.[25] And so, a wide range of Christian thinkers—not only Aristides of Athens but also Athenagoras, Justin Martyr, and the unknown disciple who sent a letter to a seeker named Diognetus, to name a few—produced ecclesial apologetics that argued for the truth of the gospel on the basis of the sustained existence and ethics of the Christian community. According to Aristides, the best explanation for practices of countercultural and counterintuitive generosity was the veridicality of the deity to whom Christians offered their allegiance. To sustain such patterns of life was to provide a living argument for the truth of the God whom Christians worshiped and the texts the church trusted. In contexts today in which the church's ethics are similarly perceived as more peculiar than our claims of theism or resurrection, perhaps it is time to appeal anew to the life of the church as evidence for the truthfulness of the faith.

Although this approach to apologetics received less emphasis after the church gained imperial favor in the fourth century, ecclesial apologetics was not completely lost. As Joshua Chatraw and Mark Allen point out, the sermons and writings of North African pastor Augustine of Hippo were rich with ecclesial apologetics.

> Given a holistic anthropology and the communal way humans think, Augustine offers us a vision for persuasion that we can use to invite others to accompany us on a journey along a new path with a new community. . . . For Augustine, the church is like an apologetic hospital for the blind and broken. It catechizes the seeker of truth. . . . The church's calling is to be a living apologetic.[26]

25. Rowan Greer, *Broken Lights and Mended Lives: Theology and Common Life in the Early Church* (Pennsylvania State University Press, 1991), 123. For more on the cultural impact of the early Christian *habitus*, see also Alan Kreider, *The Patient Ferment of the Early Church: The Improbable Rise of Christianity in the Roman Empire* (Baker, 2016), 2.

26. Joshua Chatraw and Mark Allen, *The Augustine Way: Retrieving a Vision for the Church's Apologetic Witness* (Baker, 2023), 98, 127.

Augustine repeatedly appealed to the miraculous expansion of the church as well as the consistency between the church's profession and practices as evidences for the truth of Christianity.[27]

Recent Examples of Ecclesial Apologetics

The late twentieth and early twenty-first centuries witnessed a vast expansion in apologetics resources, apologetics conferences, and even apologetics celebrities. And yet, throughout this era, there was "a troubling absence in apologetics: namely, the church."[28] The works of English missionary theologian Lesslie Newbigin represented a welcome exception to this pattern. Faced with the challenge of shifting social orders in the twentieth century, Newbigin addressed the relationship between apologetics and the Christian community in ways that echoed earlier emphases on the church as living evidence for the credibility of the faith. In his book *The Gospel in a Pluralist Society*, Newbigin asked,

> How is it possible that the gospel should be credible, that people should come to believe that the power which has the last word in human affairs is represented by a man hanging on a cross? I am suggesting that the only answer, the only hermeneutic of the gospel, is a congregation of men and women who believe it and live by it. . . . It is only as we are truly "indwelling" the gospel story, only as we are so deeply involved in the life of the community which is shaped by this story, that it becomes our real "plausibility structure," that we are able steadily and confidently to live in this attitude of eager hope.[29]

For Newbigin, the life of the church is a means by which God reveals the gospel plausible in an increasingly secular society. Faithful communities of Christians are signposts of a coming kingdom in which every assertion and ethic taught in God's word will be publicly vindicated (1 Pet 2:6–8, 12; Rev 3:9). Since the church is not merely a past artifact but a present ethical and relational reality, the life of the Christian community may provide a better starting point for initial apologetics conversations in secular contexts than any common ground found in rational arguments or historical artifacts.

---

27. Augustine of Hippo, *De Vera Religione*, in *De magistro, De Vera Religione*, ed. Domenico Bassi (Edizioni Testi Christiani, 1930), 1.1–7.12. The Greek philosophers aspired to this consistency but never achieved it; if Socrates and Plato had returned to life and glimpsed this consistency after the establishment of the church, the philosophers would have recognized the consummation of their aspirations and turned to Christ, according to Augustine.

28. Chatraw and Allen, *Augustine Way*, 97.

29. Lesslie Newbigin, *The Gospel in a Pluralist Society* (Eerdmans, 1989), 227–33.

The Practice of Ecclesial Apologetics

"It is one thing," Augustine of Hippo admitted when considering the difference between knowing the truth and putting it into practice, "to see the land of peace from a mountain's wooded summit . . . and quite another to stay on the path that guides you there."[30] It's a helpful image to keep in mind as we grow in our knowledge and application of God's truth. It's also a worthwhile maxim to recall when attempting to retrieve a concept from the ancient past. It is one thing to throw out a theory articulating why ancient ecclesial apologetics might be relevant today, but it is quite another to provide fellow apologists with a path that guides them to use this method today. Still, any theory of apologetics remains incomplete until Christians are able put it into practice in their present lives. And so, now that we've considered some biblical and historical foundations for ecclesial apologetics, my goal is to unpack two ancient ecclesial arguments to show how each example might be practically reconfigured for apologetics today. These are far from the only ecclesial arguments available to us. They are intended only as examples of how ecclesial apologetics works, not as an exhaustive accounting of such arguments.

1. An Ecclesial Argument Against Naturalistic Explanations of the Church's Initial Expansion

In the days that followed the initial proclamation that God raised Jesus from the dead, only ten dozen or so women and men remained faithful to their Messiah's memory (Acts 1:15). And yet, by the opening decades of second century, the news that a crucified Jew had returned to life spanned the Roman Empire from Syria to Spain, and at least four written retellings of his life were circulating in some of the empire's largest cities. No one knows for certain how many people became Christians in the first century of the church's existence, but it's impossible to deny the church's rapid initial expansion in response to the testimony of eyewitnesses.

The earliest defenders of Christianity saw the church's early growth and survival as clear evidences of divine power at work. "Don't you see that the more [Christians] are punished, the greater their number becomes?" one second-century apologist asked his interlocutor in *Epistle to Diognetus*.

30. Augustine of Hippo, *Confessions, Volume I: Books 1–8*, ed. Carolyn J.-B. Hammond (Harvard University Press, 2014), 7.21.

"These things do not appear to be human works; they are the power of God; they are the proofs of his presence."[31]

Augustine of Hippo developed this line of thinking into a detailed argument that treated the church's initial growth as evidence for the truth of the resurrection. According to Augustine,

> Now, we have three incredible things, and yet all three have come to pass: First, it is incredible that Christ rose in the flesh and ascended with his flesh into heaven. Second, it is incredible that the world has come to believe something so incredible. Third, it is incredible that a few unknown men, with no standing and no education, were able to persuade the world . . . of something so incredible. Of these three incredible things, the people we are debating refuse to believe the first, they are compelled to grant the second, but they cannot explain how the second happened unless they believe the third. . . . If they still refuse to believe that Christ's apostles really did work miracles to convince people to believe in the message of Christ's resurrection and ascension, they leave us with one even greater miracle: that the whole world has somehow come to believe in a miracle without any miracles at all.[32]

Not even those who rejected the gospel in Augustine's context could deny that men and women from a multiplicity of backgrounds had joined the church in response to the apostles' initial message and miracles. And yet, unless the apostles actually saw death reversed and unless God worked miracles through them, it seems unlikely that the church would have survived. Unless supernatural events actually took place, no one would have taken the apostles' claims seriously, and the eyewitnesses themselves would never have persisted in their proclamations through persecution. Thus, for Augustine, the initial rise of the church functioned as evidence for the truth of the resurrection. To acknowledge the church's initial growth without admitting the truth of the resurrection would have been to assert that the world somehow became convinced of a miracle in the absence of any miracles, which Augustine saw as absurd.

Retrieving this ecclesial argument for the twenty-first century requires contemporary apologists to consider the rise of other religions as well as potential sociological explanations for the widespread reception of the apostles' witness. In the centuries that stand between Augustine and us, historians

31. *The Epistle to Diognetus (with the Fragment of Quadratus)*, ed. Clayton Jefferd (Oxford University Press, 2013), 7.9.

32. Augustine of Hippo, *City of God, Volume VII: Books 21–22* (Harvard University Press, 1972), 22.5.

and sociologists have shown that some aspects of the church's multiplication from a few dozen faithful followers to a powerful minority in the Roman Empire might be assigned to reasons that are not supernatural. Given the rapid expansion over the centuries of religions such as Islam, this argument works only for the church's initial expansion against all social odds in the first century in response to the testimony of eyewitnesses.

Nevertheless, Augustine was right to recognize the sheer unlikelihood that "a few unknown men, with no standing and no education" could have convinced so many people unless these initial witnesses actually experienced something supernatural. Unlike Confucius and Siddhartha Gautama, who spent many years training their disciples, the teaching ministry of Jesus lasted only three years or so; unlike Muhammad, Jesus died in humiliation, with no armies, no wealth, and no heirs.[33] Yet the church grew in response to the testimony of eyewitnesses, and the best explanations of this initial multiplication point to the presence of a power that cannot be confined to natural categories. Thus the church's initial growth provides evidence for the miraculous underpinnings of the apostles' proclamation.

Evidential apologists have tended to focus on the martyrdoms of the apostles, pointing out that these eyewitnesses would have known if the resurrection had been a fabrication and no one is likely to die for a lie if they know it's a lie.[34] This argument can be effective. And yet, many listeners may not be ready to grant the historicity of these martyrdoms as common ground. By starting with the church's initial expansion against all natural odds in the first century, ecclesial apologetics takes a different route to the same truth, which reflects some of the earliest arguments for the truth of Christianity.

2. *An Ecclesial Argument Against Naturalism*

According to the second-century apologist Aristides of Athens, the church's care for the parentless and the poor could not be sustained unless the deity

33. Hans Küng, *On Being a Christian* (Doubleday, 1984), 335–46.

34. See, e.g., Josh McDowell and Sean McDowell, *More Than a Carpenter*, rev. ed. (Tyndale, 2009), 67–72. My critique is not intended to question the cogency of this argument; the argument itself is cogent and effective, and it remains valid and useful. I first encountered this line of reasoning in 1991 in an early edition of *More Than a Carpenter*, and the argument was instrumental in my return to confidence in the truth of Christianity after a season of doubt. My contention is that some of the effectiveness of historical evidential appeals may have diminished and that other approaches that include communal and ecclesial components might need to supplement, precede, or replace some of these arguments, at least in our initial encounters with non-Christians.

confessed by the Christians was real and true. This apologist wasn't alone in viewing the charity of the church as evidence for the truthfulness of the church's faith. The apologetic arguments in *Epistle to Diognetus* similarly highlight the church's habits of care for the disadvantaged.[35] This pattern persisted long past the second century. The last pagan ruler of the ancient empire complained that the church's philanthropy toward strangers was still drawing people away from the venerable gods and goddesses in the fourth century.[36]

Aristides's line of thinking was certainly cogent in its initial context. His argument may not, however, work for us in quite the same way that it worked for ancient defenders of the faith. One of the key reasons why the second-century church's charitable habits seemed unsustainable apart from divine power was because these habits were so radically countercultural in their context. Greek and Roman cultures assumed that the weak and the marginalized didn't matter. The church's patterns of generosity declared the opposite, claiming that the powerless matter no less than the powerful. Today, care for the poor, the parentless, and the physically and mentally challenged doesn't seem nearly as countercultural to us as it did to people in the second century. In contemporary contexts, even persons who despise Christianity tend to see such charity as commendable behavior.

How, then, can contemporary apologists retrieve this ecclesial argument? And how might this argument maintain its starting point in the moral habits of the church? One way to recontextualize the argument today is to demonstrate that secularity cannot provide a coherent rationale to explain why the vulnerable should be viewed as valuable. The belief that every human being is equally valuable and worthy of dignity was—as historian Tom Holland has noted—never a self-evident truth on the basis of any perspective outside the Jewish and Christian Scriptures.[37] This assertion is rooted in the self-authenticating truth of biblical revelation (Gen 1:27), and it was only through the church's proclamation of the truth of Scripture that

35. *Epistle to Diognetus*, 10.2–8. The author seems to have been responding to a query related to the love of Christians for one another ("φιλοστοργιαν," 1.1). The description of benevolent love described in 9.2 ("φιλανθρωπιας," cf. Titus 3:4) suggests the love of Christians for one another is grounded in the love of God for humanity; imitation of God's love causes Christians to reach beyond their love for one another and to love their neighbors who are not yet Christians.

36. Julian, "22: Ἀρσακίῳ ἀρχιερεῖ Γαλατίας," *Letters. Epigrams. Against the Galileans. Fragments* (Harvard University Press, 1923). Cf. Julian's usage of φιλανθρωπία ("ἡ περὶ τοὺς ξένους φιλανθρωπία") with *Epistle to Diognetus* 9.2.

37. Holland, *Dominion*, 400.

the world became convinced such a claim might be true. Christianity has undeniably failed at times to practice the biblical truths of universal human dignity and moral equality. And yet, without Christianity, no commitment to the universal moral equality of human beings would have come about in the first place.[38]

Since the notion that the vulnerable have value is ultimately grounded in God's revelation, secular narratives of evolution and social progress can never provide a coherent rationale for this conviction. From the perspective of natural selection, what contributes most to human survival is "to favor kith and kin, do down our enemies, ignore the starving, and let the weakest go to the wall."[39] And thus, even as secularists applaud charity and equality, their own constitutive narratives are incapable of explaining how these values might have evolved in the first place or why a community ought to practice such values.

Natural selection depends on the survival of the mighty and the sacrifice of the weak; Christianity is all about the sacrifice of the Mighty One for the sake of the weak.[40] This inversion of values revolutionized human history, and the ethics of care that flow from this revolution carry the trademark of the communion of the saints. Whenever a secular social order aspires to equality and charity, a system that claims to be godless is applying for a loan from the bank of the Christian tradition while simultaneously denying that the bank has any capital worth borrowing. Unreciprocated generosity toward the poor and marginalized is only perceived as praiseworthy in secular contexts today because people are still mining their values from the moral motherlode that two millennia of Christian tradition embedded in the soil of civilization.

And that's why the church's care for the vulnerable provides such vital evidence for the truth of our faith. Our churches are filled with acts of unreciprocated hospitality and generosity that reveal there must be more to the cosmos than mere matter. The family that adopts a foster child whose relational patterns have been disordered by years of abuse, the parents who choose to raise a son with Down syndrome instead of seeking the abortion their physician recommended, the woman who treats sex workers as human

---

38. Samuel Moyn, *Christian Human Rights* (University of Pennsylvania Press, 2015), 6. See also Watkin, *Biblical Critical Theory*, 385–88.

39. Anthony O'Hear, *Beyond Evolution: Human Nature and the Limits of Evolutionary Explanation* (Clarendon, 1997), 133; see also 129–32, 143–44.

40. Language alludes to Glen Scrivener, *The Air We Breathe: How We All Came to Believe in Freedom, Kindness, Progress, and Equality* (The Good Book, 2022), 64–65.

beings with dignity and helps them to forge new lives for themselves and their families, the layman who pours his life into educating inmates serving life sentences in a state penitentiary, and so many others—all these acts and more declare that naturalistic explanations of the cosmos are epistemologically and evidentially defective. Secular expressions of such generosity can be, with few exceptions, traced back to the Christian tradition, which leaves us with a strong ecclesial defense against the materialist's claim that the cosmos "is all there is or ever was or ever will be."[41]

This particular ecclesial argument doesn't get us to the truth of the gospel, but it does falsify secular narratives that claim naturalistic evolution as a universal explanation for social phenomena. When practiced by an entire community, habits of unreciprocated generosity provide an apologetic argument that calls into question every materialist account of human social behaviors. Ecclesial arguments of this sort are ideally suited for contexts where conversations are more likely to start with the impact of Christianity on the social order than with apologetics grounded in the design of God's world or the miracles in God's word. Such arguments pave the way for deeper discussions that reveal the deficiencies of naturalistic metaphysics and epistemology. Placing the church at the forefront of apologetics in this way also makes it clear to the non-Christian that embracing Jesus without entering into the life of a local church is not a viable option.

The Church Is Evidence

Of course, the arguments I've outlined here are far from the only ancient defenses that could fall within the classification of ecclesial apologetics. Justin Martyr appealed to the multiethnic unity of second-century churches as evidence of God's presence among them.[42] Minucius Felix made the case that the church's sexual mores were better and more beautiful than any ethic practiced outside the church.[43] *Epistle to Diognetus* implied that Christians

41. Carl Sagan, *Cosmos*, rev. ed. (Ballantine, 2013), 1.

42. Justin Martyr, *Apologia A*, 14. For a contemporary exploration of ways in which multiethnic and multisocioeconomic churches falsify secular narratives, see Jamaal E. Williams and Timothy Paul Jones, *In Church as It Is in Heaven: Cultivating a Multiethnic Kingdom Culture* (IVP, 2023).

43. Minucius Felix, *Octavius*, 31.1–7, in *Tertullian: Apology. De Spectaculis. Minucius Felix: Octavius* (Harvard University Press, 1931). For a contemporary appeal to Christian sexual ethics as an apologetic, see Daniel Darling, "What If the Christian Sexual Ethic Becomes a Feature, Not a Bug?," *Christianity Today*, June 20, 2024, https://www.christianitytoday.com.

are the source of life and wholeness in the world[44]—which was part of the point I was trying to make when I asked the man at the London Underground station whether he would prefer a world filled with churches or mosques.

I don't pretend that ecclesial apologetics is the only possible approach to apologetics that a faithful apologist can take. And yet, in contemporary contexts where conversations about the goodness of Christianity increasingly precede any readiness to discuss miraculous or metaphysical claims, it is vital that apologists deploy arguments that defend a Christian way of being in the world. The exit door from the challenges of secularity may not be ahead of us but behind us, in the ancient church. Now is the time to retrieve the central role of the communion of the saints, not only as a context for training in apologetics but also as evidence for the truth of the faith we proclaim. I am not simply calling for more apologetics in our churches; I am calling for more church in our apologetics.

"Epistemologically, there is no substitute for 'saints'—palpable, personal examples of the Christian faith."[45] The gathered communion of these saints is the beloved and blood-bought bride of Christ, but that's not all. This beloved communion is also a living plausibility structure that unmasks the madness and meagerness of every process of thinking that is not wholly submitted to Christ as king.

Resources for Further Reading about Ecclesial Apologetics

Jones, Timothy Paul. "'Something Divine Mingled among Them': Care for the Parentless and the Poor as Ecclesial Apologetic in the Second Century." In *Rich in Good Deeds.* Edited by Robert Plummer. Fontes Press, 2022.

Kreider, Alan. *The Patient Ferment of the Early Church: The Improbable Rise of Christianity in the Roman Empire.* Baker, 2016.

Presley, Stephen. *Cultural Sanctification: Engaging the World Like the Early Church.* Eerdmans, 2024.

44. "What the soul is in the body, Christians are in the world." *Epistle to Diognetus*, 6.1.

45. Stanley Hauerwas and William Willimon, *Resident Aliens* (Abingdon, 1989), 103. For communities as epistemology-shaping structures, see also Alasdair MacIntyre, *Whose Justice? Whose Rationality?* (University of Notre Dame Press, 1988), 7.

Scrivener, Glen. *The Air We Breathe: How We All Came to Believe in Freedom, Kindness, Progress, and Equality.* The Good Book, 2022.

Williams, Jamaal E., and Timothy Paul Jones. *In Church as It Is in Heaven: Cultivating a Multiethnic Kingdom Culture.* InterVarsity, 2023.

Responses to Ecclesial Apologetics

Classical Apologetics Response

Melissa Cain Travis

In recent years, the focus of many conversations about the viability of Christianity has noticeably shifted. As Timothy Paul Jones observes, "Challenges to the church's faith are increasingly less likely to begin with doubts about what is true and more likely to start with questions about what is good." He believes that this cultural moment in which we find ourselves is ripe for a retrieval of ecclesial apologetics, the practice of citing the truth of Christianity as the best explanation for two phenomena: (1) the church's explosive rise and (2) the far-reaching, continual impact of its ethical precepts. Related to the latter, this approach draws on the crucial fact that Christianity provides both objective grounding and the original countercultural precedent for the ethical standards that still permeate Western culture. As Tom Holland has argued, whether we realize it or not, "all of us in the West are a goldfish, and the water that we swim in is Christianity."[1]

Jones lucidly demonstrates that ecclesial apologetics enjoys both biblical and patristic support yet recognizes that it needs to be adapted for contemporary application. He models two ways in which this can be achieved. First, by comparing the birth and subsequent explosion of Christianity—which happened against multiple odds—with the circumstances surrounding the origin and historical expansion of other major religious systems such as Buddhism and Islam. The differences are quite striking, but the key question is whether a nonbeliever will become open to divine providence or instead cling to some sort of social evolutionary blanket theory (most, if not all, of which beg the question in favor of naturalism). In such a case, the apologist—especially one who is not well read in cultural anthropology—would have to resort to a different tactic.

The second ecclesial argument Jones reconfigures for modern utility is, in my estimation, the more powerful option. He points out that intrin-

1. Andrew Brown, "Tom Holland Interview: 'We Swim in Christian Waters,' " *Church Times*, August 5, 2024, https://www.churchtimes.co.uk.

sic human value and equality are not self-evident; they require external grounding, which Christianity provides in its doctrines of God and humankind. Secularists have no adequate ontological foundation for these moral ideals; the material stuff of the world and the processes by which things develop and operate cannot ground the intangibles we hold so dear. A naturalistic evolutionary theory may, to one degree or another, account for physical traits and behaviors, but then it hits a categorical brick wall; matter in motion cannot dictate moral truths or duties. In short, naturalism is simply unlivable in any consistent sense. This problem is central to the standard moral argument for the existence of God. The ecclesial argument goes a step further by showing that Christianity has provided ethical particulars upon which our society was built, and that they are still widely embraced; as Jones puts it, "People are still mining their values from the moral motherlode that two millennia of Christian tradition embedded in the soil of civilization." This is a compelling line of argumentation that, in my experience, has broad appeal; it captures the attention of anyone who harbors strong moral convictions about human value, equality, and justice. A worldview that is not only livable but distinct in ways that have led to the flourishing of humanity is attractive, and as Christians strive to follow Christ, others will take notice of our uniqueness in this dying world. "Faithful communities of Christians," Jones explains, "are signposts of a coming kingdom in which every assertion and ethic taught in God's word will be publicly vindicated."

The conclusion that ecclesial apologetics is necessary for a time such as this, when the *goodness* of Christianity is what many have placed in the dock, is certainly justified. As Blaise Pascal understood, a worldview often must be shown to be desirable before the case for its truth will be heard.[2] "A growing number of non-Christians are willing and able to consider the question of whether the church is good for the social order long before they're able to make sense of our arguments for theism or the Trinity or an empty tomb," Jones writes. Thus, as with cultural apologetics, ecclesial apologetics may sometimes be the wedge that opens the door, but many will still desire additional reasons to believe that orthodox Christianity's primary theological claims are indeed true. With that said, perhaps ecclesial apologetics is best regarded as an integral part of a holistic approach. As with cultural apologetics, it has great potential to be helpful in many conversational scenarios, but it is not always the most appropriate stand-alone strategy. This is by no

2. Blaise Pascal, *Pensées*, trans. Roger Ariew (Hackett, 2004), 9 (S46/L12).

means a weakness; as with even the most versatile tools in an "essentials" toolkit, it is precisely what is needed for certain purposes. Beyond those, it is often valuable in complex projects that require multiple tools.

Evidential Apologetics Response

Sean McDowell

This chapter starts with a compelling evangelistic interaction between Timothy Paul Jones and a man in London. There are a few positive takeaways from this exchange alongside his suggested model of ecclesial apologetics. First, Jones asks questions. Rather than simply making arguments, he leads with questions. The Gospels and Acts reveal Jesus asking 340 questions; the letters of Paul include 262 questions.[3] Any effective apologist today must similarly engage others with questions. Second, and more related to his suggested apologetics approach, Jones emphasizes the importance of the church rather than the individualism that often characterizes modern evangelicalism. In our individualistic age, Jones's focus on the testimony and defense of the corporate church is commendable. Third, Jones is right that distinct Christian living not only puts detractors to shame but also provides evidence that God is working through the church. The church's distinct moral practices proclaim to the world that there must be more to the cosmos than mere matter. When we live Christianly, our actions support the claim that Jesus has risen from the dead and reigns over creation. Living in such a manner gives authority to our proclamation of the gospel and defense of the faith. And yet there are some areas I would challenge too.

1. Where is the evidence that moral issues should replace or precede truth-related claims?

Jones writes that "the life of the Christian community may provide a better starting point for apologetics in secular contexts than any alleged common ground found in rational arguments or historical artifacts." I agree that the life of the Christian community *may* provide a better starting point for apologetic encounters. He models that with his opening exchange. Yet I am not convinced it is the primary approach we must adopt. I find no convinc-

3. Bob Tiede, *340 Questions Jesus Asked* (2024) and *262 Questions Paul the Apostle of Christ Asked* (2022), https://www.leadingwithquestions.com.

ing evidence to back up the claim that "conversations about the goodness of Christianity tend to precede debates about metaphysics or the miraculous claims of Scripture." While this may be true in *some* cases, where is the evidence it is true in *most*? Before changing our apologetics approach, we should demand clear evidence that conversations about God have shifted so radically in this direction and that beginning with an ecclesial apologetic is most effective.

Whether because of supposed misogyny, genocide, slavery, or homophobia, there does seem to be an increased emphasis today on moral critiques of the Bible. Yet where is the evidence these issues have replaced (or need to precede) truth-related claims? Challenges against the reliability of the Bible persist, and in my experience, these are often the first issues nonbelievers want to discuss. While Jones may be right that questions regarding the goodness of Christianity loom large with many non-Christians, I hesitate to make sweeping generalizations that such conversations must *precede* claims about truth.

2. Has the negative perception of the church today been underestimated?

While Jones recognizes that Christians have often failed to live out their commitment to dignity and moral equality, I suspect he may have underestimated the negative perception of the church today. Some recent books have argued that America is not only a *post*-Christian culture but an *anti*-Christian culture.[4] Incessant news stories about the failures of pastors, apologists, and other Christian leaders have undoubtedly contributed to this perception. While it is important to highlight the good that Christians have done throughout history and to argue that human rights depend on a Christian ethic, given that society has seen its public failures, it is questionable whether our most effective strategy is to argue for the presence and power of God behind the church.

3. Is the expansion of the church the most convincing argument for the resurrection?

Jones cites the example of Augustine, who considered the explosion of the church as evidence of the miraculous underpinnings of the apostolic con-

4. For examples, see Aaron M. Renn, *Life in the Negative World* (Zondervan, 2024); and Rosaria Butterfield, *Five Lies of Our Anti-Christian Age* (Crossway, 2023).

fession to the resurrection. Jones may be right that this is a line of defense apologists need to develop further. And yet I have not seen any evidence that *this* is the most convincing argument defenders of the resurrection should embrace. Where is the proof it works with nonbelievers? I teach a graduate level course on the resurrection, and students consistently rate the willingness of the apostles to suffer and die as one of the most compelling evidences for the resurrection.[5] Interestingly, Islam is poised to become a larger religion than Christianity by 2075.[6] If current trends continue, and Islam outgrows Christianity, should we then affirm the truthfulness of Islam? This question highlights the weakness of relying too heavily on an ecclesial apologetic.

In sum, ecclesial apologetics has an important role to play in *defensive* apologetics. If someone argues that Christianity has been a force for ill, then we need to highlight the fruit of the Christian faith and emphasize that human rights and equality themselves depend on Christian commitments. Yet ecclesial apologetics has limits when applied *positively*. It seems far easier to give a naturalistic account for the positive contributions of the church than for the historical facts of the resurrection.

Presuppositional Apologetics Response

James N. Anderson

Timothy Paul Jones provides an eloquent and persuasive case for ecclesial apologetics, which contends that "the presence and power of God [provide] the best explanation for the existence and ethics of the church" and thus "the

---

5. Jones cites an early edition of *More Than a Carpenter* as introducing him to this argument. While my father and I included this argument in the 2009 edition of the book as a result of my doctoral studies on the fate of the apostles, we have since modified the argument in the latest edition (2024). Importantly, the willingness of the apostles to suffer and die for their faith does not prove the truth of the resurrection, but it does indicate their sincerity that Jesus rose and appeared to them (i.e., they were not liars). It is part of a larger, cumulative case for the resurrection of Jesus. In my experience, people still resonate strongly with this argument. Why? While it is easy to virtue signal on social media about what one believes, the willingness of the apostles to suffer shows they really believed it and put themselves in harm's way to proclaim it. They staked their lives on the resurrection of Jesus and suffered because of it.

6. Don Feder, "Islam Poised to Become the World's Largest Religion," *Washington Times* (January 1, 2023), https://www.washingtontimes.com/news/2023/jan/1/islam-poised-to-become-worlds-largest-religion/.

life of the church is itself a key evidence for the truth of the faith." Gratifyingly, I found much to affirm and little to disagree with in Jones's chapter. I agree that we find support for ecclesial apologetics, as Jones defines it, in the New Testament (Matt 5:16; John 13:34–35; John 17:20–23; 1 Pet 2:12). He points especially to Peter's first epistle, where the apostle exhorts believers to bear faithful witness to "the hope that is in you" both with *words* ("make a defense [*apologia*]") and with *deeds* ("your good behavior in Christ"). Furthermore, as Jones amply documents, there is strong historical and theological support for ecclesial apologetics in the lives and writings of the early church fathers.[7] This is an ancient and deeply rooted tree that has borne considerable fruit. Jones rightly observes that our cultural moment is ripe for a revival of ecclesial apologetics. We do indeed encounter more and more non-Christians who dismiss theistic arguments and Christian evidences with a shrug of the shoulders, because they fail to see what difference it makes in their own lives and in the world they inhabit. The embodied witness of the gospel-transformed people of God can reach and move hearts in a way that merely intellectual appeals often cannot.

Jones offers some helpful practical application of ecclesial apologetics with his arguments against naturalistic explanations of the church's initial expansion and naturalistic evolutionary accounts of modern secular values. In sum, it seems to me that virtually everything Jones says about ecclesial apologetics is compatible with the presuppositional approach I defended in my chapter.

Despite these happy concurrences, I nevertheless want to raise some critical points. These are not offered as objections to ecclesial apologetics *as such*, but rather as invitations for clarification, refinement, and further dialogue.

1. We cannot mount an argument from the life of the church without reference to what the Bible says about the identity of the church.

Central to ecclesial apologetics is the idea that "the life of the church" can serve as persuasive evidence for the truth of Christianity. However, this presupposes that we can *identify* the church in the first place. Who or what counts as "the church"? Where are we to look for the relevant evidence? Roman Catholics have their answer, the Eastern Orthodox have

7. I would add that we also find support in the later Protestant Reformed tradition, as reflected for example in the *Westminster Confession of Faith* (1.5): "We may be moved and induced by the testimony of the church to an high and reverent esteem of the Holy Scripture."

theirs, evangelical Protestants have theirs, and so on. Presumably, it is only the *Christian* church that gives evidence for Christianity. But how do we define "the Christian church"? I assume that Jones, as a fellow Protestant, would agree that the (true) church is defined by God's word. In that case, we cannot properly identify the church *independently* of the authority of Scripture. There is thus a kind of two-way testimonial relationship at work (albeit an asymmetrical one, since Scripture alone carries divine authority). Scripture defines the church, and the church evidences the truth of Scripture. This underscores what presuppositionalists have contended about the need to defend "Christianity as a unit"—as an integrated holistic worldview. We cannot mount an argument from the life of the church without reference to what the Bible says about the identity of the church.

"NO TRUE SCOTSMAN" FALLACY

Also known as "appeal to purity." Informal logical fallacy in which a claim is challenged, and the claimant responds by limiting the claim to examples that meet a standard set by the claim. The most common example of the fallacy is:

ARGUMENT: "Ach! No Scotsman puts sugar on his porridge."

REPLY: "But my uncle is a Scotsman, and he likes sugar with his porridge."

REBUTTAL: "Ah yes, but no *true* Scotsman puts sugar on his porridge."

Unless the challenger can be shown to have had an incorrect understanding of the major term, this rebuttal is fallacious because the appeal to purity modifies the definition of the major term.

2. *We may find appeals to the life of the church are a double-edged sword.*

If the good character and sacrificial love of Christians are evidence *for* Christianity, then do the (often heinous) moral failures of Christians serve as evidence *against* Christianity? To his credit, Jones acknowledges the "inevitable question [of] Christian hypocrisy" and answers with Justin Martyr's argument that professing Christians living in unrepentant sin are not actually Christians. An uncharitable critic might accuse this response of committing the "No True Scotsman" fallacy! A more charitable take, however, would be to say (with presuppositionalists) that some degree of circularity is legitimate and unavoidable within the context of a self-defining and self-justifying worldview.

3. *We may have to make a selective appeal to the ethics of the Christian community to press the apologetic argument.*

Ecclesial apologetics holds that the ethics of the Christian community (ethics both preached and practiced) and the historical societal reforms motivated by Christianity are evidence of its truth. I agree—but then, I'm a Christian! Christian ethics are attractive and conducive to human flourishing from a *Christian* perspective, but many modern unbelievers see things quite differently. Christian views on abortion, marriage, and sexual purity, for example, strike them as backwards, bigoted, oppressive, and unjust. No doubt they appreciate *some* Christian values, such as caring for the poor and the marginalized. But now it looks like we have to make a *selective* appeal to the ethics of the Christian community to press the apologetic argument.

4. We need a holistic and flexible apologetic that can offer compelling responses to both apatheism and antitheism.

It's true that many unbelievers today aren't interested in rational arguments for theism or historical evidences for the resurrection. Yet many still are. Some of them are influential skeptics and critics of Christianity with significant followings on video-sharing platforms and social media. We need a holistic, flexible apologetic that can offer compelling responses to *both* apatheism *and* antitheism. Ecclesial apologetics makes an essential contribution to that task. I see ecclesial apologetics not as an *alternative* to presuppositional apologetics but as a *complement* to it, one that emphasizes the evidence of God's sanctifying power at work in his church through the ages. Perhaps, then, Jones and I can join forces in promoting "ecclesial-presuppositional apologetics"!

Cultural Apologetics Response

D.A. Horton

We live in an age in which testimonies of church abuse and scandals flood our social media feeds, leaving many individuals angry, scared, and traumatized. Sometimes, it appears that the light of the gospel of Christ has been overshadowed by the poor stewardship of the gospel by those entrusted to embody its principles while spreading it to the world. In solidarity with a cultural apologetic method, Timothy Paul Jones presents a redemptive apologetic approach inspired by a time when the global church was not in a position of sociopolitical power and influence.

Grounding one's apologetic methodology in Christ's church ensures its longevity. The church is the only entity this side of eternity guaranteed to remain in existence until and beyond the triumphant return of Jesus Christ. This truth should motivate all members of the global church to heed Christ's call in Revelation 3:2, "Wake up, and strengthen what remains and is about to die, for I have not found your works complete in the sight of my God" (ESV). In doing so, Christians of today and tomorrow would do well to align themselves with the countercultural lifestyles of their spiritual fathers and mothers such as Aristides of Athens, Justin Martyr, and others that Jones cites.

Jones points to the global church's testimony throughout history as an argument that reveals the insufficient coherence and rationality of natural selection, particularly as this relates to justice for marginalized groups. This perspective has equipped me with valuable discussion points when conversing with naturalists about their concerns regarding human welfare. Particularly in collectivist and marginalized communities, this innate longing for justice, bestowed by God, is too significant to overlook. Referencing the testimony of the global and historical church strongly resonates with their hearts, minds, and lived experiences. Cultural apologetics uses this same way of thinking by referring back to the specific social teachings of Jesus before presenting historical and current examples from the global church.[8]

My soul was deeply encouraged while reading Jones's references to Augustine's African ethnicity and to the early church's powerful witness that brought together both women and men in communities marked by cultural, ethnic, and generational diversity. This evidence also resonates with the approach of cultural apologetics, highlighting the tangible recognition of the image of God in every person.

The greatest concern I have with ecclesial apologetics is not with the method itself or even with the treatment given here. My anxiety spikes only as I consider that the greatest challenge to the application of ecclesial apologetics is the stubborn and hardened hearts of those whom Christ has redeemed. In a time of increasing polarization not only between non-Christians and Christians in North America but also among those professing a shared faith in Christ, a united ethical witness to the power and presence of God seems to be a cultural mountain many will not be willing to climb together due to differing opinions on economic, political, racial,

8. For a list of specific social commands given by Jesus, see D.A. Horton, *Intensional* (NavPress, 2019), 174–76.

and social issues. Yet, along with Jones, my hope remains rooted in Jesus's own prayer for us:

> I do not ask for these only, but also for those who will believe in me through their word, that they may all be one, just as you, Father, are in me, and I in you, that they also may be in us, so that the world may believe that you have sent me. The glory that you have given me I have given to them, that they may be one even as we are one, I in them and you in me, that they may become perfectly one, so that the world may know that you sent me and loved them even as you loved me. (John 17:20–23)

Acknowledgments

The portions of this book that proceeded from my pen were written at Blackwell's Bookshop on Broad Street in Oxford and in the café at the British Library in London. Many thanks to President R. Albert Mohler, Provost Paul Akin, Dean Hershael York, and the trustees of The Southern Baptist Theological Seminary for their generous allowance of a writing sabbatical in England that enabled me to complete this project. The chapters from my fellow contributors were edited in a somewhat more mundane yet still delightfully caffeinated location, Sunergos Coffee on Willis Avenue in Louisville.

I am even more grateful now for Melissa Cain Travis, Sean McDowell, James N. Anderson, and D.A. Horton than I was when the project began. Hall of Fame baseball player George Brett once described a "Dirt Disorder" that afflicts players after they stop playing baseball.[*] His point was that if you're not regularly performing a task under pressure, it's easier to criticize how well others accomplish that task. The further you get from the dirt of the baseball diamond, the more likely you are to disparage those that are still laboring in the dirt. This disorder isn't limited to baseball. I've met more than a few strong proponents of particular apologetics methods who suffer from Dirt Disorder too. These scholars are dogmatic and harsh in their critiques of other apologists, yet they themselves are not consistently sharing and defending the gospel among ordinary people. One of my goals in assembling this group of contributors was to avoid this disorder. I wanted apologetics practitioners who are engaged day-by-day in the messy work of doing apologetics. Now, at the completion of this work, it is my delight to report that the project has been free from Dirt Disorder. All of us have disagreed with one another about apologetics methods, but each disagreement has been marked by humility and collegiality. As I see it, one of the reasons for this amicability is because each contributor spends significant time in the "dirt" of practical apologetics. This practicality is apparent on every page of *Understanding Christian Apologetics*. My prayer is that what captures the hearts of readers is not any particular apologetics method but the truth of God that apologetics defends.

Timothy Paul Jones

*Joe Posnanski, *The Baseball 100* (Simon & Schuster, 2021), 261.

Contributors

James N. Anderson (PhD, University of Edinburgh) is the Carl W. McMurray professor of theology and philosophy and academic dean at Reformed Theological Seminary in Charlotte, North Carolina, and an ordained minister in the Associate Reformed Presbyterian Church. He is the author of *Paradox in Christian Theology* (2007), *What's Your Worldview?* (2014), *Why Should I Believe Christianity*? (2016), and *David Hume* (2019), in addition to many scholarly and popular articles on topics in Christian apologetics and philosophical theology.

D.A. Horton (PhD, Southeastern Baptist Theological Seminary) is the director of Intercultural Studies at California Baptist University, where he is an assistant professor. He also serves as an associate teaching pastor at The Grove Community Church. With several authored books, two planted churches, and nearly thirty years of experience in urban ministry, D.A. is unashamed to embrace his God-given call as a missiologist dedicated to North America. His published works include *DNA: Foundations of the Faith* (2012) and *Intensional: Kingdom Ethnicity in a Divided World* (2019).

Timothy Paul Jones (PhD, The Southern Baptist Theological Seminary) is the C. Edwin Gheens professor of Christian family ministry, director of the Center for Christian Apologetics, and chair of the Department of Apologetics, Ethics, and Philosophy at The Southern Baptist Theological Seminary. He is author or editor of more than a dozen books, including *In Church as It Is in Heaven* with Jamaal E. Williams (2023), *Why Should I Trust the Bible?* (2019), *How We Got the Bible* (2015), and *Misquoting Truth* (2007). He serves as a preaching pastor at Sojourn Church Midtown and cohosts *The Apologetics Podcast*.

Sean McDowell (PhD, The Southern Baptist Theological Seminary) is associate professor of apologetics at Talbot School of Theology, Biola University. He is the bestselling author, editor, or coauthor of over twenty books, including *End the Stalemate* (2024) and *Apologetics for an Ever-changing Culture* (2025). He speaks internationally on issues related to culture, apologetics, and worldview. He is the cohost of the podcast *Think Biblically* and has a popular YouTube channel.

Keith Plummer (PhD, Trinity Evangelical Divinity School) is dean of the School of Divinity and professor of theology at Cairn University in Langhorne, Pennsylvania. He previously served on the pastoral staff of Our Saviour Evangelical Free Church in Wheeling, Illinois. Keith is a fellow of The Keller Center for Cultural Apologetics. He hosts the *defragmenting* podcast and is published in *Before You Lose Your Faith: Deconstructing Doubt in the Church* (2021) and *The Digital Public Square: Christian Ethics in a Technological Society* (2023).

Melissa Cain Travis (PhD, Faulkner University) is a fellow at Discovery Institute's Center for Science and Culture, where she teaches continuing education courses on science, faith, and philosophy. She has a PhD in humanities with a concentration in philosophy, in addition to an MA degree in science and religion from Biola University and a BS in general biology from Campbell University. She is the author of *Thinking God's Thoughts: Johannes Kepler and the Miracle of Cosmic Comprehensibility* (2022) and *Science and the Mind of the Maker: What the Conversation Between Faith and Science Reveals About God* (2018).